IRVING
STREET
& OTHER HARTFORD
MEMORIES

Dennis Sullivan

Cover Photo: the Lorenzo family, 51-53 Irving Street, Hartford,
CT,
Summer, 1933. All Photos: The Russo, Testa, Lorenzo,
Sullivan family collections.

For Barbara

Acknowledgements

Make no mistake, this book was a collaborative effort. Accordingly, I wish to acknowledge and thank those indispensable people who so generously contributed information, assistance and encouragement, chief among them: Timothy Hlavaty of Riverside, California and Rod Dornan of Wethersfield, Connecticut, longtime friends, who both did yeoman work on the manuscript in progress and whose many suggestions brought this undertaking to fruition; friends and the very helpful staff at the Hartford History Center, Hartford Public Library: Martha-Rea Nelson, Eileen Colletti, James Santa-Mo, Elena Filios, and Brenda Miller; the staff of the Connecticut Historical Center; family members who shared details and anecdotal stories: my sister, Eileen McCall; Aunt, Ann Ostiguy; Uncle through marriage Frank Scelza, Cousins, Donna Nardi, Paul and Robert Ostiguy, and Linda Wilchinski; friends: Bob DiGreggorio, Judy Simon Klemba, Ed Drydol, Mike Angelillo, Tom Shea. Peter Hawkins, Joe Cassano, Jr., Bob Countryman, Bobby Knight and Murray Cohen; and finally a special thanks to another friend, Andy Wert, and my Sister-In-Law, Pat Tracy, who offered great encouragement when this project was just a twelve page prototype. Thanks also go out to: Steve Thorton, James Johnson and David Ryan Polgar for their input. And, as always, my loving wife, Barbara, who has assisted me in all things, this being just another.

I owe a very special debt to my brother-in-law, Bob McCall, for editorial and technical assistance without which this book would not have been completed. A big thanks, Bob.

Contents

Preface

You may find ghosts of the old days anywhere you go in the North End of Hartford, CT, provided you know where to look and your heart is in the right place. I have no trouble uncovering ghosts of people and places in my former neighborhood around Irving Street. They will always be there and I will always look.

There are brand new houses where some older ones once stood. Number 39, once the proud domain of the Owen Johnson family whose welcoming veranda sheltered scores of neighborhood kids for over a decade for board games in summer's heat and rainy days, and whose backyard saw many snow forts, has been replaced by a home that sits cockeyed, sideways on the lot, one side now being the front.

Likewise, the old Phillip's three-decker, at 46-48 and directly across from my family home, was removed for a newer version. In the original version, I can still see Mr. and the biddy Phillips, whose brother Sam, 48, hung himself in its cellar after the stock market crash in 1929. They are sitting out on their second floor porch spying on neighborhood kids, launching tirades against any who dared tread on their lawn or phoning the police when we played ball in the street. Or in my own old backyard, the five-car garage, built in the 1920's, and my grandmother's pride and joy. It's long gone, down to the ground leaving a concrete slab large enough for a basketball court. How many times my cousins Paul and Bob and I scampered across that rooftop.

Here and there, bushes, hedges and trees, still survive including, somewhat miraculously, the two maple trees of my childhood that stood in front of my house at number 45. But many of the lawns have disappeared and with them landscaping in general. My grandmother's carefully manicured yard home to many varieties of flowers—Hydrangeas, Iris and roses, bushes, a large vegetable garden out back and a peach tree no longer around. No more root hole filled with her annual harvest and covered with branches, ready for extraction all winter long. Then too, Mrs. Maule's beautiful flower garden in the rear of her prized single-family home, nonexistent, the fir trees out front also vanished. Today's landscape is a more urban blacktop, once greenery, masking a way of life that's no more.

Few would now recall that for many years at the beginning of our street near Homestead you could easily make out the once imposing Veeder-Root factory across the New York, New Haven, Hartford Railroad tracks--three stories tall and occupying a city block. Fewer would remember that during WWII our neighborhood was guarded by an anti-aircraft piece atop Veeders and manned by an Army boy. Or that when the company parking lot on Homestead was empty on weekends or holidays it served as an asphalt playing field on which to hone our baseball skills.

For years we lived next to Patsy Pietro, an unforgettable character, operating pigeon and homemade rabbit cages in his backyard, carting scrap wood for their construction in a self-made wheel barrow from God knows where, now a forgotten figure. Yet I can still visualize him, burly, bent and disheveled, trudging his way down the street pushing a full load inside his contraption.

Or how about Harry O'Neil, a WWI vet who once lived at number 11 with his three brothers. He was cited for heroism in January 1919, after plunging fifty feet into an icy Thames River while on a bridge job to save a 14 year old co-worker only to have the lad die the next day because he hit his head in the fall. Even our heroes fade away with time.

Then too, in 1922, and a fact largely forgotten, famous Metropolitan Opera singer Rosa Ponselle came to town to sing "Oh Promise Me" at the wedding of Rosalind Goldstein then residing in that same Irving Street house, once occupied by the O'Neil's, now having moved away. And into the first floor at number 9 more than two decades later, my childhood buddy Hertzel Rotenstein came to live with his family after surviving the Nazi death camps and Holocaust in World War II Europe.

Mary and Tom Grady grew up across the street at number 6. Mary married Tom Meskill and became First Lady of Connecticut; her brother Tom, had his minesweeper sunk off the Philippines in January 1945, survived and came home safe and sound.

And probably nobody now recalls Alden Grout Davis, a veteran of the Army of the Potamac, of number 17 who died at eighty-two in October of 1919.

Across from my house diagonally at number 44, Rose Yush, a secretary at Weaver High School and a widow, lived and raised her son Ed for several years in her mother's house. Her husband David Yush, a Marine and former All District Quarterback at Weaver, was killed on Saipan on July 4, 1944 - Outside of the family, does anyone still know or care about their sacrifice?

Think of the buzz when one day Sophie Tucker, "the last of the red hot mamas," showed up on the block to visit a friend or when the King Sisters arrived at my grandmother's home in the early 1940's to drop off their kids for babysitting by ma and her sisters while they drove off to perform at aunt Ella and uncle Joe Russo's Club Ferdinando in the south end.

My ghost hunting could take me around the corner of Albany facing downtown--- who can forget Izzy and Ida Pomeranz, parents to two future college professors, who lived in a large house next to the Atlantic Station and not far from their business, the Pomeranz Bakery where my mother would send me for her favorite, turnovers of various flavors, rye and pumpernickel breads and fresh rolls with seeds.

Does anyone now remember the elderly Jewish couple, Sally and Leon Steinhaus, operating World Tailors, or the smallest First National on the planet next to the Garden Restaurant on the corner of Garden, John the barkeep presiding? In the 1940's,my dad earned extra income there as a part time bartender on weekends but who knows whether it was more work or pleasure? I had my first swig of beer at the Garden, when just eight years old and hated it.

On the other side of Garden, Bill Harris' Harris Pharmacy with its awesome soda fountain and swivel chairs, Classic Comic Books selection, movie, and detective magazines, sundaes and ice cream sodas. Backtracking and crossing the avenue heading to the west, you could not miss the stately Goodwin Tavern at the corner with Irving, circa 1810, with its six chimneys and ten fireplaces. It was removed forever for a Dunkin' Donuts parking lot in the 1950's, today, however, an asphalt landscape. Close by, I can still feel the crush of the weekend hordes crowding the original Crown Market near Magnolia or the excitement I felt watching early TV in the window of the TV-Radio store near Vine, just some of dozens of Albany Ave. establishments no longer with us.

At the corner with Burton, there was Morris Pharmacy owned and operated by my friends Harry and Morris Feldman, a WWII vet and 1936 graduate of Weaver High, who when I was an undergrad opened their door to me after-hours for open ended bull sessions. I remember those evenings any time I pass by and wish the brothers were still around to welcome me one last time. Instead, while the building still stands, there's no sign that this once vibrant neighborhood establishment ever existed.

Moving back down to the corner with Magnolia who could ever forget those delicious aromas from *Platt's* Deli, the pastrami and kishka, seducing passerby and customers alike.

Returning to Irving Street, our old neighborhood, one block away, who will remember the generations past of the children there: Judy, Howie and Bobby Simon, Billy Dixon, Eddie Yush, Junior Johnson, Bobby Zabel, Henny and Harriet Solomon, Bobby Maule, Mary Jane Cahill, Jeannie, Jackie and Bobby Morris, Carol Del Greco, Ellen O'Hare, Hertzel Rotenstein, Ellen and Steve Kahn, Mary and Joan Williams,

Danny Larensen, Frances "Tootsie" DeLucco, Santos (Sal) Style, Bob and Jerry Strouch, Rose Marie and Adele Urrichio, Peggy Slicker, my cousins Donna and Linda St. Pierre, my sister Eileen, or during the summers, the Woodhouse kids, and briefly, Tommy Rush.

It is gone. The William's sisters and Tootsie jumping rope, Rose Yush, out on her veranda, calling for Eddie, Owen Johnson, Sr., pulling his car into the driveway after work, Murray's mother Mrs. Cohen, slowly making her way toward the corner and to her job at Pomeranz Bakery, Jerry our longtime mailman delivering the mail, the Hartford Times, our afternoon newspaper, arriving.

All gone.

Irving Street, Looking South

On the Move

Our blue 1936 Dodge was packed, idling and ready to go. On the back seat and floor boxes of bric a brac, frying pans and other utensils sticking every which way, barely room for a little guy my size and no one else. Mom and my kid sister Eileen sat comfortably in front while I stood on the running board outside, taking one last look around. Meantime, Dad raced inside at my biding, ("Daddy, daddy, my boat...") trying to locate a missing in action toy PT boat. I took another hard look at the burned empty lot two houses over and thought about the recent excitement when half the Hartford Fire Department showed up to put out a raging bush fire. Nearby sat the trash barrel shed where my dad not long ago smashed a rat with a shovel while I watched from afar slightly agog. Memories of three years on upper Edgewood, years when my sister had been born and I learned some of life's most basic functions of walking talking, eating - life outside the crib. But today was moving day and I was anxious to get going—our destination 45 Irving Street, a mile away.

The place we were moving to had been bought at auction by my Italian grandparents for about eleven thousand dollars in 1940. Since that purchase we had been waiting patiently for the call from my grandmother that a rent was available. It took longer than anticipated but at long last the call came and things were set in motion--movers called, packing begun, right down to this our deadline moving day.

Dad came back empty handed and gave me the bad news--my PT was still missing in action. Ready to go, he put the car in gear and eased us down the driveway one last time turning left on Vine heading south. Along the way we passed Vine Street School, built

13

20 years before and strictly ruled by Mrs. Wheelock, principal of my soon to be first school. Shortly thereafter, the site of our own first apartment lodging a few years before at the corner with Mather, flashed by. At that point, my father faced two choices: a left turn down Mather and then take Magnolia, or Upper Irving but instead he decided to continue down Vine. Soon we came upon a section of power lines, fallen during the Hurricane of 1938 and traversed by my mother with me in utero on her way to see my grandmother. A frightening thought. Finally, there were the apartments where my friend Maxine lived.

We turned east at the light at Albany aside the most imposing landmark on the whole avenue, the Horace Webster Congregational Church completed thirty years before, transplanting the steeple and columns from the old Fourth Congregational on Main Street. We glided along over the trolley tracks, soon passing one of my father's, uncle Jimmy's and Grandpa Michael's favorite haunts, the Golden Oak Tavern, with the cane backed chairs, next to Platt's Deli where we got our cold cuts and rolls anytime we went visiting on Sundays. On the next corner at Magnolia, we passed Friedman's Grocery where I would soon be a regular, hooked on the ice cream, pops and candy. A few doors further, Weinstein's Funeral Home appeared, before turning right (the street then being two ways) at the gas stations on the corner of Irving and finally creeping into our driveway, four houses down on the right.

Our arrival was something of a homecoming for my parents, as both sets of my grandparents, Irish and Italian, lived next door. In 1943, the Lorenzos, my Italian side, owned both houses, living on the first floor of 51-53 themselves, and renting the second to the Sullivan family (their tenants since the early 1930's. Originally, five Sullivans lived on the upper floor—my grandparents, Uncle Jimmy, Frank, my dad, and Aunt Peggy. Abbey Sullivan, 56 years old, the grandmother I never knew, had died a decade earlier. My mom and dad connected and married four years afterward, both leaving the nest for the first time. Then, brother Jimmy soon followed suit and married. This left Aunt Peggy (a.k.a. Peppi) at home to care for her aging father, sacrificing herself. That was the way it was then.

Downstairs was home to three Lorenzos in 1943. There was my grandmother, Lillian, (Nonni), grandfather Dominic (Dadone)—both well into their sixties--and Aunt Vera (a.k.a. V) who was in her late twenties, still single, and contributing to the war effort working at the

Veeder Root factory around the corner. Just the year before, in fact Aunt V made it into a Hartford Courant photo with a co-worker in downtown Hartford showing the public what they did on the job for the war effort. The other five Lorenzo girls were married by that time and off on their own, with two living in apartments on Garden, the next street over.

In the middle of World War II, Irving Street was a peaceful, tree-lined neighborhood of mostly two family homes sandwiched between Homestead and Albany Avenues. Considering what was happening elsewhere in the world, it was a safe haven. No one was bombing our houses, invading our city, killing, transporting, torturing, spreading mayhem, a great blessing indeed. Sure there were blackouts, victory gardens, rationing, worries about old man Winters, who lived two doors over, being German and all, and for both my older cousins Carl and Vic who were in uniform overseas, but by and large the war remained far away.

Seventy years later, Irving Street is viewed by urban planners and city hall as a part of Upper Albany, but back when we moved in it was simply part of the north end, just to the west of Clay Hill. Vine Street School, Jones Junior High, and then Weaver High, a mile away, were the designated public schools. St. Joseph Cathedral School on Asylum Hill was our parish Catholic school, though some like Frances DeLucco opted for St. Patrick Grammar School, downtown.

Our new home had two maple trees providing shade in the front and one in the back, especially of value in those days before air conditioning. It also boasted a wonderful veranda that spread across the front, wrapping around the side near our front door. There was grass and hedges, bushes and some flowers. We occupied the first floor rent. Our front door was half glass, half heavy wood. The outer wall to the hall hosted a beautiful stained glass window that was in vogue when the house was built forty years before. The rooms were fairly spacious, except the children's bedroom to the right rear overlooking the driveway. It could only be described as tiny, just managing to fit a single bed for me, a crib for Eileen and a small dresser. To increase the claustrophobic feeling, there was light from only one window. The bathroom was also shrunken, with a sink, toilet, radiator and a bathtub. It would be many years before we experienced the luxury of having our own shower and it was not on

Irving Street. In the meantime, we made do with a short rubber hose connected to a shower head and screwed into the faucet.

The kitchen had a gas stove with a kerosene attachment on back, a washing machine for clothes, a refrigerator which we still called the ice box, a few wall cabinets, a table, chairs, sink (one half of it deep for washing clothes by hand with a washboard), linoleum flooring and a small pantry. Every room had a radiator and most were wallpapered. My parent's bedroom was big enough to fit a queen size bed, dresser, highboy, and hope chest along with two closets. The dining room housed a couch, a small fold up table for special occasions and a built in the wall china cabinet. The living room was modest with the usual easy chairs, tables, lamps and a Duncan Phyfe style divan with a reproduction of a painting of Stratford on Avon hanging from the wall above it.

There also was also a good sized front room. Closets were small. Our heat was coal fired, delivered by way of a chute through a cellar window. Our radiator pipes groaned and creaked at night. We did not yet own a telephone, nor a fan for relief from summer heat. On the worst days, mom closed all windows and blinds and pulled down shades, survival skills she learned growing up on the eastside.

Out back, a twenty year old five car garage painted blue straddled the yard, leaving only a two foot alley way along the south side. My dad rented the center garage space. Crushed rock covered most of the yard out back. The driveway along the side of the house had two concrete tire tracks with a strip of earth running down the middle. A swath of grass ran the length of the side of the house, beginning at one of the maple trees. We had a small back porch, with a lilac bush next to the stairs, leading into a hallway entry. The second floor tenants entered from the opposite corner near the driveway. An odd assortment of battered trash barrels were set against the back wall and had to be firmly covered as rats were constantly lurking. There was also a garbage container, operated by foot, buried in the ground.

Magnolia, the next street over to the west and behind us, was mostly composed of single and two family homes, also built during the Homestead Park boom days. Like Irving, it had another half across Albany Avenue. With only one exception, all the property lines facing Magnolia were divided by fences or hedges. Our yard didn't have any because the garage sufficed as a divider. The rear of my grandparent's home had a three-foot wood fence running across and wire fences separated properties on one side, serving as a kind of trellis for Nonni's rose bushes. Many homes were also sectioned off in the same way. From the backyards of houses across the street, you could see the apartment buildings on Garden Street, the edge of the Clay Hill District.

At first there weren't many kids my age around. Immediately next door to us, however, there was a large family named Morris with several older kids—Ann, Rita, Jeanie, Jackie, Chuckie and Bobby. Ann and Rita, the oldest, were already part of the work force, Chuckie was in trade school. Jackie was starting out at Weaver. Jeanie, nearly a teenager, and Bobby, a big, burly pre-teen, attended St. Joe's Grammar School on Asylum Avenue. Mrs. Morris was a very affable, large woman, married to a very small physical specimen, Charles Morris, a factory worker at Veeders. Mom struck up a friendship with her fairly quickly and I became In awe of the Morris boys who were all strong and very athletic and could shimmy down the back porch posts from their second floor dwelling. As the boys advanced in age and left home, I became the beneficiary of toy rifles, a b.b. gun, football helmets and other hand me downs. And daughter Jeannie signed on as a readymade baby sitter for us.

There was no committee to welcome us. Eventually, Aunt V came out on the front porch as we unloaded and yelled to mom, "Hey Rosie, ma's knocking five dollars off the rent." Such discounts were unheard from my grandmother who kept a tight fist with the pocket book.

Back then our street brought forth accents and words from many different places—Irish, Italian, French, Eastern European, Jamaican, Greek, German, and New England Yankee, the last being the Johnson family two doors over. Mrs. Johnson was descended from the Holcomb line, prominent in Hartford County. Prim and proper, Mrs. Maule, living in a single family toward the middle of the street, was a well-known dress maker of Jamaican Heritage, who saw a constant flow of customers at her door. Her son Bobby was the Hartford Times paperboy personified, holding his empire until almost 19 years old, when it got divided up allowing me to inherit the Irving Street route, four years into the future. At number 20, Dominic DeLucco, owner of a local bar and grill and the future first Italian Mayor of Hartford, lived on the second floor with his family and daughter, Frances (a.k.a. Tootsie), a tomboy, who became a good friend growing up. Mr. Winter, owner of the house on the other side of my Grandparents, struck fear in me early as he was rumored to be a Nazi sympathizer. But during the war, anyone of German extraction was probably considered suspicious. Finally, let's not forget Grandpa Michael Sullivan, that grand old Kerry man, who sounded like Barry Fitzgerald, the Hollywood actor, or my Italian grandparents who seldom spoke in English.

That same year, my dad Frank Vincent Sullivan born and bred in Hartford, celebrated his thirty-fifth birthday. Dad was a proud graduate of St. Patrick School near the church downtown and St. Thomas Seminary High School, then on Collins Street, placing at the top of his class. Known to friends as Sully, his childhood neighborhoods encompassed years on Avon and Kennedy Streets, rough and tough ethnic streets on the Eastside where brass knuckles sometimes flashed on Halloween, or so he told me. Thirteen years earlier, the Sullivans had moved into 51 Irving Street, becoming the Lorenzo's first renters there, setting the stage for my parent's upstairs-downstairs courtship.

Dad was considered by some in the Sullivan family as quite a catch. My great aunt Katherine called him "handsome and brilliant" and thought my mom not worthy of his attention. "Frankie can do better," she criticized. Moreover, there was the story that some relatives in the old country were so awestruck by a photo of my dad that they prayed to it. (Certainly, this had to be a pagan tale) When dad met mom, however, he was twenty-six and not getting any younger.

As the older, unhappy woman, mom—known forever to my sister and I as ma--already twenty eight and had seen a younger sister, Laura, married off the year she started dating Frankie. She was short, skinny and practically blind without her thick glasses. Ma's childhood was cut short in seventh Grade, age 13, when my grandmother sent her off to work, first in tobacco sheds, then to sweat shops, like Wiley, Bickford and Sweet Corp. It was the close up work in the sweat shops that started her vision deteriorating, or so my mother complained, harboring bitter feelings toward her mother for not buying her glasses when she needed them. As I said, my grandmother's purse strings were very tight.

Rose had a penchant for song writing, (none ever published), and verses salvaged from that time may have expressed her mood:

"Gonna sleep off all my worries

Dream all my blues away

Don't wake me up tomorrow

Unless it's a sunny day."

Oh Dad, poor Dad, my Nonni didn't make things easy, did she? His downstairs future mother-in-law Lillian had a litmus test for anyone daring to date one of her daughters: "Are you for real or for fool?" (in broken English). No record existed of my father's reply but that encounter probably got his Irish up. On another one of their dates they went to the Lenox Theater, the neighborhood movie house at Albany and Sterling. In the middle of the movie, Dad had a tonsillitis attack and had to rush himself to St. Francis Hospital. When their courtship dragged on for three years, my mom told me in her waning years, that she "put it to him." They were married in June of 1937 at St. Patrick Church, Hartford with a reception to follow in the backyard of 51-53 Irving Street.

My Sullivan grandparents came to the U.S. aboard The Cymeric, making landfall In New York City on St. Joseph's Day, March 19, 1901. They arrived with the minimal amount of money required by U.S. Immigration, about sixty dollars, according to the ship's manifest. One of my grandfather's sisters lived and worked in Hartford and was at the docks to greet them. She helped them find a place to live at 76 Avon Street, their first new world home. Life for immigrants on the Eastside was not easy. Though Michael could read and write, he spoke with a heavy brogue and the best he could land for employment was as a laborer with the Hartford Water Works which he did until retirement. The Sullivans saw four of their seven children die either in infancy, or early on, including John, 9, who fell to his death from a moving trolley.

The Lorenzos didn't arrive until April 24, 1906, sailing on the Byron out of Rio de Janeiro. Both my grandparents were illiterate and spoke little English. Their first American home was at 471 Front Street, near the Connecticut River. It was a teeming ghetto crammed with cold water flats where a person could conceivably freeze to death in winter and roast in the summer. Family owned businesses of all kinds dominated the neighborhood. Outhouses provided relief. Public bath houses were available for showers. In her autobiography, vaudeville star, Sophie Tucker, who grew up on the east side, remembered as a teenager stuffing newspapers inside her clothing to ward off the cold when she prepared her family restaurant to open in early morning before school.

Irving Street began at Homestead Avenue and continued on until it was cut in half by Albany Avenue, then continued slightly uphill to Mather. A large Veeder Root Factory employee parking lot emptied into Irving Street at quitting time in later afternoon, interrupting any on-going kid's ball games for a while. Right around the corner from us on Albany almost everything we needed was at our fingertips—a doctor, a dentist, drug stores, taverns grocery stores, delis, gas stations and auto repair, cleaners, barbers, shoemakers, restaurant, a diner, funeral parlor and even a five and dime. All right there. And right at the corner of our street trolleys still stopped, soon to be replaced by buses. There was a stop at the corner of Irving and another at Garden.

Our street and all those cross streets between Albany and Homestead up to and including Cabot were the brain child of James Goodwin who around the turn of the twentieth century gobbled up acres of land and created the Homestead Park Corporation. Until then there was little of anything west of Garden Street. In fact it is probably safe to say that if you stood at the corner of Albany and Garden in 1898 and looked west you would be looking at acres of what was up until then farm and pasture land. The Goodwin Tavern and adjoining barns would be visible nearby, as would the James Batterson house at 1 Vine Street. There would be no landmark like Horace Bushnell Congregational Church for another decade. And possibly off in the distance on a clear day the Northwest District School at Woodland and the Adams Tavern and outbuildings, McGurk's Blacksmith Shop at Blue Hills Avenue, plus a scattering of homes might be visible. Homestead Avenue was created to run parallel with Albany and also the Connecticut Western railroad tracks to the south. Irving, Magnolia, North Huntington (later renamed Burton), Sigourney, Melrose (later called Edgewood) and Cabot were developed. Furthermore, the old Goodwin Mansion on Sigourney was repurposed as a clubhouse and a nine-hole golf course was created between Sigourney and Melrose. Such was the optimism of the developers.

A bridge was constructed over the railroad tracks on Sigourney. The electric trolley car system had already been expanded into north Hartford, expediting growth. In a sales piece published in 1902, many of the original completed and sold houses are shown surrounded by a pretty barren landscape aside from a few young trees. Within two years, however, optimism faded and developers publicly were lamenting having to auction off lots and not getting what they considered a fair price. Described in sales pieces of the times as cottages, single family homes were selling for $3,500, two family homes for $4.500.

As laid out, Irving Street was roughly the length of two good sized football fields. There were five single family houses interspersed with nineteen two family structures. Although the front yard always seemed adequate growing up, they were in fact only thirty three feet wide and the distance from curbside to porch was a mere twenty five feet. This was the uniform code for all dwellings on the street. The original sidewalks were designated as four foot wide North River flagstone, much different than the concrete pathways of today's world. During the years of my boyhood, it was estimated that one hundred and eighty souls lived on Irving Street at any given moment.

Figure 1: Uncles 1944, Jimmy Sullivan, Leon Ostiguy, Sam Testa, Frank Sullivan

Kneeling: Vic Polce, Dennis Sullivan (Author)

Vine Street School

That fall (1943), Dad walked me by the hand a few streets to Vine Street School, on my first day. It didn't go well. I hadn't been exposed to many other kids outside of my cousins. Besides, school scared me. Class was already in session by the time we arrived. The teacher greeted us in the hall and tried to put me at ease but I kicked up quite a fuss--so much so it was agreed that perhaps we should try again the next day. So the next day I returned and this time I stayed. I was to remain at Vine Street School for two sessions of kindergarten (morning and afternoon) and then first grade.

My parents entrusted Cousin Vincent Testa, who was nine at the time and lived around the corner in a Garden Street apartment, with getting me to school. Vincent, a.k.a. "Deedy," was such a good kid and always looked out for me. And he could swim, play baseball, race in the Soap Box Derby and sing. I was so fortunate having him and my cousin Jerome, 3, who lived right above him in the same building, so close. The rest of my mother's large family was close enough that most major holidays and some Sundays all my cousins would visit my grandparents next door, making it possible for lots of fun and games.

When Vincent came to my house to pick me up for school, he would back up to our front stairs and loaded me onto his back, piggyback style and away we'd go. I don't recall how long or how far he managed to carry me but that's how we started out. He taught me to always walk two blocks to the crossing guard at Vine Street and then crossover. No shortcuts, as Albany was always a busy thoroughfare. Kindergarten is a blur in my mind but I do recall doing a lot of fun activities, including making a bus out of brown paper and building blocks. We were very proud of our finished construction; it being big enough to sit in and take turns driving.

After school, I started running with a pack of kids, mostly boys, my age down Vine with a girl named Maxine who we delighted in taunting with:

> "I see London,
>
> I see France
>
> I see Maxine's underpants."

With this, we would run up to her and try and flip her dress up.

Vine Street School was heated by coal like most of our homes and sometimes deliveries would be left piled in a large heap in the schoolyard, until ready for use. One night in winter it snowed and the coal got buried. This mountain of snow and coal quickly became a wonderful hill for sliding down before school and at recess. Oh, the delight of it, until after a while teachers shooed us inside.

In first grade, I was assigned a classroom toward the front of the building overlooking Vine Street. I quickly became friends with an Afro American boy named Gary Cooper who sat directly behind me. I thought his having the name of a movie star was just so cool. We played together a lot at recess and sometime whispered to each other in class. He sat directly behind me and our conversations started getting me in trouble with the teacher and vice versa. One day leaving school he invited me to join him and his friends walking home. The next thing I knew we were bolting across backyards, over fences and trash barrels. At one point, I stumbled and hit my knee and tore my pants. Gary and friends took off leaving me over near Enfield Street but of course at that age I had no idea where I was. Somehow I slowly worked my way down upper Irving to Albany directly across from my street. In the meantime, since it was now well past four o'clock a family all-points bulletin had been posted for me and my poor cousin Vincent, taking blame for my disappearance, headed out from my house to try and find me. He didn't have to go far. As soon as he reached the corner, he spotted me on the other side of Albany. Albany had a lot of traffic in those days, including large city buses, making the crossing difficult. We yelled back and forth. At last, when a slowing of traffic developed, Vincent kept his cool and successfully talked me over to the other side.

I still hadn't learned my lesson about Gary and his posse. On another day we wandered down Magnolia Street and things really began to get out of control fast. Naïve me, these boys who I thought were friends turned on me and started taunting, and stalking me. I don't remember how we got across Albany but once we did they were still after me. There were three or four of them at my heels as I neared Irving. I hoped they would leave me at my corner, heading for their own streets. Seeing they weren't about to let me go, I prayed they would finally give up when I got to my house. I was wrong and scared. They actually chased me into my backyard and wouldn't leave until ma came out and scolded them. My friendship with Gary ended at that moment. He and his friends didn't know how lucky they were that it was ma who turned them away and not my grandmother Lillian, next door, who would have given them the fright of their young lives.

In the spring of that year, I invited a friend from school over to my house to play. Our back porch led into an enclosed hallway, just outside the back door leading into our kitchen. It was one of our favorite place to play and where some toys and comic books got stored. The friend, who was a girl, and I ended up doing show and tell of our sex organs to each other. Right in the middle of our exploration, my mother, who somehow sensed from the kitchen that things had gone quiet, caught us in the act. The poor girl was made to feel embarrassed and sent home. Ma must have made me feel I had done an evil deed, because I don't think I ever spoke to my friend again.

As if things could have gotten any worse that year, not long after this I strayed into a wildly overgrown empty lot at the corner of Mather Street and Vine and caught my first case of poison ivy.

Figure 2: Vincent Testa

Figure 3: Cousins, Paul Ostiguy, Vincent Testa, Bob Ostiguy

The Circus Fire

July 6, 1944 was very hot. My dad had his day off from work and was helping get my sister Eileen and I ready for one of the great moments in our young lives—Ringling Bros. Barnum and Bailey's Three-Ringed Circus was in town and we were going. Little did we know or even suspect this event would turn into one of the great tragedies in local and my own family's history.

The day before, daddy had taken us for a sneak preview. We watched excitedly as circus workers, aided by the elephants, raised the tents. And, I still recall seeing a baby elephant pee in front of us, a truly remarkable happening to my five year old mind.

On the big day, ma, sis, daddy and I piled into our 1936 Dodge for the ride back to the circus grounds on Barbour Street, about a mile from our house. Because of the heat, daddy cranked up our front windshield a little, allowing some air to pass through, making the trip more bearable. Once there, we lucked out and got street parking a block away on a side street. Others were having to pay to park on people's lawns.

As prearranged, we met up with relatives—Aunt Amy Montano and her son, cousin Jerome, 3, and my favorite cousin, Vincent Testa, 10, along with my Aunt Ella Russo. Vincent's parents were working as was Uncle Joe Montano and couldn't attend. Ella had purchased eight tickets for us—six in one area, two in another. Childless herself, she was always doting over her nieces and nephews. Getting these tickets was more of the same.

She was my godmother, but she was more like a fairy godmother to us kids.

Like scenes from a movie without a soundtrack, we moved in slow motion up the fairway, gawking at side shows and pausing to feed elephants. For some unknown reason, however, the beasts weren't taking our peanuts, a mystery greatly frustrating to us. Vincent was wearing a white sailor's outfit with a flap on the back of his shirt plus shorts. I had on a short sleeve shirt and shorts. Being of the same age, my sister and cousin kept to themselves as we walked.

The only sound I recall from that day was that of the barker near the main entrance, hyping the show: "Step right up, Ladies and Gentlemen...."

By this time, I had become so excited that I announced I needed to use the bathroom. Daddy took me to the nearby men's room. (*It was very close to the men's room that they say the fire started which gives me pause now, years later, thinking that a half hour before I had been in that same area with daddy—the point of origin.*)

Inside the big top, it was decided that daddy would take me to occupy the two odd seats we had tickets for, high up in the northwest grandstands. I remember them as somewhere between the center ring and the one with the wild animals which was a little to the left. The rest of the family were to the right of us but not nearby.

We settled into our seats, the show began and I was quickly mesmerized by just about everything going on especially the lions and big cats act. At some point, my focus shifted to a group of Army boys, some bandaged, others on crutches, casualties of the War, occupying a section across the way diagonally. To my five year old mind this was as fascinating as the wild beasts causing me to briefly lose track of the show.

My mind swung back to center ring as the Flying Wallendas started their ascent and it was about then that I finally got a Coke which I was busy slurping. No sooner had I taken my first sips when I, along with everyone else, began noticing a small tongue of fire on the tent just to the left of the Army guys. As we watched, this seemingly harmless blaze quickly turned into a raging monster and very soon the beast was heading our way with lightening speed. I dropped my Coke and climbed onto my dad's back. In just seconds, we found ourselves with thousands of others running for our lives. It was that quick.

Strangely, I have no memory of any screams or shouts, only a sucking sound that I assume was the fire devouring air as it raced toward us. It was mostly like a silent movie which I remember in color.

To get out, we had to pass over the runway for the wild beasts, which was about four feet high and narrow, creating an instant bottleneck for hundreds of people. Daddy either tripped or was pushed down there, with the fire pressing down on us. We had about six minutes to get out alive. An anonymous man helping people picked us both up in one full swoop and threw us over the runway to the other side. One of my most vivid memories was landing on the ground and looking back to see a large tent pole ablaze come crashing down near where we had just escaped.

(*Many times I have wondered who that man was and if he survived the fire.*)

We exited the northeast, back exit, just as time was running out for the big top. About then, I recall asking my father if we should get to a firebox and sound the alarm. Of course, on that score, there was no need to worry. Many alarms had already been sounded and as we worked our way around to the front of the Barbour Street lot, we learned the fire department was already at the scene.

Daddy began the search for our family members. We worked our way back up the fairway as far as possible to a position no more than one hundred feet from the big top front entrance. It was there that I witnessed a gruesome scene no five year old, no person, should ever have to see: blackened bodies, smoke pouring from them, dragged out onto the grass and left. Daddy had to be shaken, with still no word of our loved loves.

Almost as soon as we arrived there, the Hartford Police forced us from the area so the firemen and rescue workers could function. As we reached Barbour Street, a hysterical woman approached with a young boy about my age who had a minor burn on one hand. She pleaded for daddy to help. But my father had just come away from the nightmare outside the big top, shaking his head, and told her to

"Get the hell away from here. Go to a doctor's office and not bother people trying to help serious cases." We never saw them again. It was the first time I heard my father utter what was to my young mind a swear and the thought of it has lived with me all these years.

Soon afterward, we met up with one of my aunts who broke the news that all of our family had escaped safely except for cousin Vincent. Apparently in the chaos inside they had lost him. A split second decision had been made to let him try to get out on his own. He's young and athletic, they thought, he can make it out on his own. They never saw him again. In another decision, they approved dropping Eileen and Jerome successfully from the top of the stands into the arms of a man who was helping out.

A short time later, we found ma lying in an overgrown lot next to our car, sobbing inconsolably:" We can't find Vincent, we can't find Dee Dee."

Late that afternoon and late into the evening, Vincent's father, Sam searched frantically everywhere for his only child with no success—McCook, then the City Hospital, Brown School, Even the next day's edition of the Hartford Courant, listed him as still missing. It wasn't until the last bodies were brought in toward the end of the day that Sam would find his son, identifying him by the athlete's foot he had contacted on one foot. His body had been discovered near the stairs over the animal runway in the northwest section of the big top and brought to the State Armory, serving as a morgue, for identification. My poor cousin had been trampled.

From the moment we got home, we were put to bed that night early. At some point we were advised that Vincent had died but were not allowed to attend the wake for him. It was the way of the world then; spare the children; above all, don't scare them.

It turned out to be impossible to shelter us. If anything, we were inundated by Circus Fire stories. After all this was the biggest tragedy in the history of Connecticut. Then too, because of our proximity to our grandparent's house next-door and it being summer with the windows up we could hear all too well the screams, sobbing and cries of anguish. In addition, many of the kids at school that fall had also been in attendance and it became a popular topic. Boy Scouts, in particular, bragged about cutting their way through the canvas and helping save others. None of the talk would go away, then or now.

In the months following, Vincent's mother, Aunt Laura, almost suffered a nervous breakdown over the loss of her son, especially when school resumed that fall. My uncle came home and found her perched at the front window of their second floor Garden Street apartment, hoping to see Vincent return home from school. Hearing of my aunt's profound grief, my uncle's employer, Beatrice Fox Auerbach at G.Fox Co. dispatched her own private duty nurse to be with my aunt. She stayed two weeks. Finally, at the orders of her doctor for a change of scenery, the Testas moved in temporarily with my aunt and uncle Russo who lived in a house across from Keney Park on Edgewood Street.

My father never spoke much about that day and died six years later. The Testas moved on to have two daughters and lived full lives well into their eighties. Late in my Cousin Jerome's life, he broke the news that his mother, Aunt Amy, had been pregnant with twins on the day of the circus and had lost them through a miscarriage. In a bizarre twist in my own life, a dozen years later, I was present in a hanger fire at an Air Force Base, realized I had to get out fast and did. The hanger burned to the ground in ten minutes. My mother never forgot July 6th and often said, "Every time I see a sunset it reminds me of the fire."

Figure 4: Christmas at Nonnie's, circa 1960's

Christmas Italiano

(A Montage)

Each Christmastime in the mid-1940's, in those years just before the end of and immediately after WWII, all roads for our family ended at my Italian grandparent's house, next door. It was a tradition that had started mostly in the 1930's with the marriages of several of the Lorenzo daughters—my mom being one-- bringing with it a motley collection of uncles—French Canadian, Sicilian, Italian and Irish. And it had expanded over the previous decade with the birth of children---my cousins. Christmas was big doings for the Lorenzo clan.

Looking back to those times, is like revisiting pages from a long-forgotten book. Open a page and out pops my curly-haired little sister Eileen and I setting out for Nonni's, right after dinner. I was wrapped up in my Navy P-coat, scarf, mittens and hat with earflaps, sis wearing her snow suit and of course arctics. It had been snowing steadily since noon. Blazing a trail through the snow, we arrived on our grandparent's front porch and were immediately bedazzled by our Aunt Vera's annual Christmas masterpiece— a large tree with bubble lights—seen through the living room window. Taking our breath away, however, wasn't the tree but the huge stockpile of presents stacked underneath--huge because my mother's very large family stockpiled many presents here for the holidays.

Due to the storm and holiday, the gas stations at the corner with Albany Avenue shut down early. Veeder Root's Factory at the other end of our street sat quietly, darkened except for maintenance lights. The soldier and anti-aircraft gun stationed atop the factory during the War were gone, having been recently removed.

Our reverie was almost immediately interrupted by the crunching of the footsteps and jangling of loose change. Up the walk our Hartford Times newsboy, Bobby Maule trudged, still out collecting, even during the storm. He was unusually quiet for this festive night but the storm appeared to have taken something out of him.

Soon Aunt Vera,(a.k.a. V,) stuck her head out of the half open storm door, looking puzzled, chuckled: "Hey, Bobby, what are you doin' out on a night like this?"

"Collecting," he announced nonchalantly. Our Aunt, who was never one to mince words, fired back, "Yeah, well you must be nuts. Does your mother know you're out?" She started to say something else but stopped. Instead she invited us all into the hallway. Stomping our way in, we followed Bobby and began shedding our snowy clothing.

Aunt V returned with her dark blue change purse and counted out the money due along with the obligatory Christmas tip. Then, with her tip dangling in one hand, she deftly pulled out a small bag of candy wrapped in red cellophane and gold ribbon with the other. "I think this is what you're looking for?" she mused. Bobby's eyes warmed for the first time. He politely accepted his treasures and was quickly off to his next stop, slipping and sliding down the walk. At the turn off, he looked back and waved to us, then disappeared into the storm.

For our first order of business inside: scrutinizing the bonanza of presents under the tree, our main reason for showing up early. I reviewed all of them, breaking them down into categories: Ours vs. Theirs, Mine vs. Hers, Big Ones, little ones, Noisy ones, Heavy vs. Light, odd shaped packages, all swell.

Next, we migrated to the candy dishes seeking out hard Christmas candies. We pranced around sucking the sweet and stickiness from our fingers, light headed. It was well past 7:30 now with still no sign of anyone else arriving, no surprise given the weather.

Flip another page in this book to a scene of heavy snow burying my grandparent's front yard, the street nearly unpassable. It turned out to be after eight o'clock before the first of my relatives, the Ostiguys from West Hartford, pulled their Chevy into the driveway.

Without much adieu, the back door to their car jerked open and my Cousins Paul and Bobby charged out, plowing into the snow. This was the moment I'd been waiting for and I was quick to get dressed and join them. The boys were close in age to me, Paul being half a year older, Bobby roughly a year and a half younger. Because of the closeness of the Lorenzos, we were together a lot, especially for holidays and birthdays.

On this night, Bobby was running interference for his brother, then switching off as they headed toward me.

"Get him," Paul yelled playfully and the chase began; staggered into a snowdrift and tried to run but my cousins, always athletic, were too quick for me. Before I knew it, we were wrestling and tumbling in the snow, over and over, until we finally ceased nearly exhausted, laying outstretched.

Before long, their father, Uncle Leon, not a man to be taken lightly, appeared on the porch and commanded: "C'mon in the house before you catch pneumonia."

We got up and started moving toward him but are slowed by one last round of snowball throwing. My uncle was still standing there, arms crossed, and fuming. We'd seen that look from him before so this time we complied. Marching like little soldiers, we passed in revue by my French Canadian Uncle who popped us a last minute salute and then slapped Cousin Bobby playfully on his butt "Get in there," he growled and laughed.

Once inside the front hall--home to Aunt V's prized collection of miniature animal statues, housed in a mahogany, glass door cabinet--we quickly turned flush from the rise in temperature. We piled everything—hats, gloves, coats, boots in one snowy pile there.

We entered the living room through a glass door and immediately passed a black, upright, Baldwin player piano to the right with a plastic Santa and reindeer running across the top. There was the typical couch, easy chair, tables and lamps. The Christmas tree stood in the middle of a three-windowed alcove to the right. At the opposite end of the room there was a marble fireplace, not in use. French doors opened into the dining room. On the radiator cover by a side window rested a nativity scene. In various locations there were Christmas candies and fruitcake. After paying homage to the tree and gifts, just as we had my cousins made a bee-line for the candy.

Out in the kitchen, Aunt V was occupied baking pizzelles, an Italian waffle-like creation. As the evening wore on, she'd be cooking large Italian sausages. V was always busy.

Nonni's kitchen led into a pantry with built-in cabinets also including a refrigerator. The room contained furnishings and equipment of the 1940's—kitchenette table and chairs, double sink, gas stove and washing machine. Actually, It was a room full of doors. Besides the porch door, there was a back door, half wood and half glass with a bell attached that could be rung from the hall by twisting.

In that same back area, a door to the left took you into my grandparent's bedroom. Along the inside wall near to the kitchen table another door led into Aunt V and Uncle Armand's bedroom.

V and Armand were our newlyweds, my Uncle having returned from the War in Europe. He was a French Canadian who had grown up in Frog Hollow during the Depression. On the outside wall, there were two doors—one leading into a very small and only bathroom, the other into a side sun porch. On the floor nearby, sat my Grandfather's spittoon. Finally, there was the door between the kitchen and living room which was festooned from above with mistletoe.

Like his bride always on the go, Armand has been running around constantly, taking coats and hats and setting out a bottle of anisette and glasses for company as they arrived. He was also appointed to mix high balls for the adults. At this point, he had a big smirk on his face, as if he knew something no one else was aware of, especially the children. Armand had anchored himself under the doorway with the mistletoe, something it was quite possible he himself had hung there earlier.

My Uncle loved to put on a show and tonight was no exception. Without hesitation, he reached up, fondling and caressing the mistletoe. His eyes were locked on V as he called out to his bride, "Well?!" Hearing this, my Aunt did a slow playful dance across the floor and ended up giving him a big smack on the lips, designed to add to the show. She then raised a pizzelle hot off the stove to his lips. "Manga," she offered. Armand took a large bite after which they kissed again.

In walked Uncle Joe and Aunt Amy (a.k.a. Mimi) Montano and son Jerome, my sister's contemporary, having driven from their Garden Street apartment around the corner-- normally walking distance but tonight difficult. Uncle Joe was short and pudgy, an auto mechanic by trade, whose constant companion was a stogie. He also liked to play the Joker with kids. His hand shot out to me saying, "Merry Christmas, Murphy." On still other occasions he substituted McGillicuddy for Murphy. Once he greeted me like this, Joe was in his element. He chagrined me to no end. "Sullivan, it's Sullivan," I insisted. But my protest got me nowhere. (*Incredibly, this gamesmanship was to last another four decades.*)

A few steps behind Uncle Joe appeared Mimi who gave me a very loving hug and kiss and went straight to the kitchen where my Grandmother was about to hold court around the kitchen table. She was a sweet tempered woman who enjoyed kidding around.

The Ostiguys were already inside. Aunt Ann (a.k.a. Ziz), was the designated family piano player and singer, who had taken voice lessons as a young woman and ached for a career on the stage. She played by ear and belted out songs in the style of Sophie Tucker, "Last of the red hot mamas." However, instead of life on the wicked stage, my grandmother hired her out to Veeder Root's Factory with her sister V where she met and married another factory worker Leon Ostiguy, my other uncle of French Canadian blood, who was a few years younger than her, much to her embarrassment. They had two boys and a girl--Cousin Judy and her brothers, Paul and Bobby. Ziz also headed for the kitchen and a rendezvous with my Grandmother, with little Judy trailing.

Though small in stature, Leon owned a grip of steel. And like most of my uncles, he was full of mischief. I was fearful of his handshake, which he would always apply with a devilish smile. "Merry Christmas, Butch," he chirped reaching out to me. The shock of his grip instantly set me reeling. I remember struggling to stay afoot. Emotionless, he stared me down searching for my reaction, at the same time applying more pressure. Throughout my ordeal, he kept a straight face. I grimaced, finally crying "ouch" before he released me. Almost immediately, his hand shot out another invitation. This time I declined.

Minutes earlier, the Testas had showed —Aunt Laura, Uncle Sam and baby Claudia. Sam sported a grey fedora, covering his baldness. He was fond of hats and like his brother-in-law, Joe, he loved to chomp on a stogie. "Gosh damn snow…almost got us killed. Annabelle didn't like it." Annabelle was one of the many pet names my uncle gave his cars. Laura said her hellos and exited for the kitchen where her sisters and mother waited to view the baby. This child, the Testas first since losing Cousin Deedy in the Circus Fire, generated special interest around the table and was passed from sister to sister and eventually my Grandmother.

A decade earlier, Sam landed in Hartford as a very young race car driver (Number 88) on the national circuit. His older brother Phil, also a racer, had moved here earlier from Kansas City, Missouri in the late 1920's and settled for good after being involved in a racing accident at Charter Oak Park, West Hartford.

At the time of Phil's arrival locally, brother Sam was little more than a teenager still living at home in the midwest. The Lorenzo girls had read of Phil's mishap in the local press—following the story about a poor Italian boy hospitalized far from home, with great interest. They visited him at the hospital and upon recovery he became a favorite visitor at 53 Irving Street. Soon he was sending snapshots of the Lorenzo girl's home, usually group photos. Young Sammy was awestruck by the photos, one of the sisters standing out above all others. "That one's for me," he announced unequivocally, pointing to Laura Lorenzo.

In the early Thirties, Sam pulled up stakes and followed his brother east on the national racing circuit, ending up in Hartford where he fell madly in love with Laura resulting in their marriage in 1933. Phil wed Frances, my aunt's good friend, and both brothers ended up settling here, never more to leave.

Along with the Testas, Aunt Ella Russo, only recently a widow, made her appearance. Ella was the family dynamo, a free spirit decked out in a mink stole. Though short like ma and Nonni, she more than made up for what she lacked physically by sheer force of personality. Her eyes, one of her strong points, sparkled for the gathering, creating a noticeable lift in energy. Everyone gravitated towards her. And Ella loved the limelight. This second generation immigrant daughter, born in Brazil who had grown up poor on the eastside, the friend and sometimes confidante of politicians, entertainers, athletes and business people. Auntie Ella was also my Godmother. On this eve she carried with her an 8X10" photograph of her hobnobbing with friends at Sloppy Joe's Bar in Havana, Cuba. It was quickly being passed around and viewed.

This Christmas she was forty-two years old and a character. Without much fanfare, she began strutting her stuff for the amusement of all, especially the young." Oh, you'd better watch out, you'd better not cry, better not shout, Aunt Ella's telling you why, Santa Claus is coming to town…He knows if you've been good or bad, so be good for goodness sake." as she sang, she cavorted about.

On the go, she pointed at each of us and asked, "Have you been naughty or nice?" By now I was starting to feel guilty about the naughty part, the good Sisters of Mercy having grilled us thoroughly at school daily about the dynamics of the sinful life. Maybe this would not be such a good Christmas after all, for buckaroos.

A moment later, I noticed my Uncle Emil and Aunt Mary Polce removing their coats. Emil was a stocky man, born in the old country. He survived the European battlefield in WWI and still owned his U.S. Army rifle, gas mask and helmet at their Crescent Beach cottage to the delight of us boys. Following the war, he had worked as a coal miner in West Virginia until blown into the air in a mining accident, souring him on mining. After this, he migrated north to Connecticut and settled in when he married ma's oldest sister, Mary. Eventually he chose a career in auto repair, opening a large garage on Cabot Street in the North End specializing in Cadillacs, LaSalles and Oldsmobiles. Emil Polce & Sons became so successful that it managed to attract celebrity clientele such as Willie Pep, World Featherweight Boxing Champion and Michael O'Shea, Hollywood actor, and husband of Virginia Mayo, a well-known film star of the 1940's.

Emil loved the sea, fishing and boating. He still spoke English with an Italian accent, even after many years here. Aunt Mary, born in 1897 in Brazil, extended me an old country greeting, "Buon Natale," Dennis and gave me a very loving hug. She was a sweet woman and never missed niece's and nephew's birthdays with a card in the mail. The Polce's had two sons—Carl, recently married, after returning from the U.S. Army and the War in Europe and Victor, a U.S. Navy veteran of the Pacific War.

Putting on a show for the kids, Aunt V popped her head out the kitchen door and loudly inquired of Uncle Emil, "Do you believe in

41

Santa Claus?" To this Emil burst into a chuckle and answered in Italian, "Santa Nicole!" as if revealing some long lost secret.

My uncles, grandfather and dad parked themselves in the living room. The smell of White Owls, Chesterfields, Pall Malls, Camels, Lucky Strikes and Old Spice permeated the room. If house rules allowed, Dadone would have lit up his favorite pipe but after years of harassment from Nonni, he knew better. She only allowed him to smoke in the cellar, poor man. My father had no such restriction and quickly was puffing away, even though doctors had already warned him about the dangers from his severely blocked arteries.

For entertainment we relied on ourselves, mostly, though occasionally Aunt V would get out her record player and spin a 78 rpm or two. We kids acted out and produced our first Nativity play. All of us were Catholic school pupils well-schooled in the story of the birth of Jesus. We used some clothesline and sheets for our curtain a doll for baby Jesus. Eileen had brought along a doll for the Christ child. Paul took over as Joseph and Jerome volunteered to play Mary. Eileen and Judy were angels and Bobby and I shepherds. When the curtain was about to go up, we shushed the crowd into quiet as we acted out our parts, bringing down the house with our singing "O Little Town of Bethlehem."

Aunt Ziz followed up with Act Two—a piano sing-along which we all loved. She knew all the favorites—Jingle Bells, God Rest You Merry, Gentlemen, Rudolph, White Christmas and many more. This was followed by Bobby playing his version of Chopsticks which made me jealous, since I couldn't play by ear like him. Dadone brought out his concertina, which he only played infrequently since his youthful days on the Brazilian coffee house scene, and treated us to an old Italian song.

This music fest was capped by Emil and Nonni performing a duet of a vintage Italian song from way back, perhaps to the time of Garibaldi and recalled by my Grandmother and Uncle. We strained to hear my grandmother's raspy voice, the first and last time I recall her singing.

Afterward, ma and her sisters headed for the kitchen again pulling up chairs around the table with Nonni at its head. We followed them in. Hearing them gossip, reminisce and cut up in English and Italian was a big moment for us growing up.

What stories they could tell.   On this occasion, my mother, the smallest of the Lorenzo girls at five feet and weighing under one hundred pounds, led things off, "Strict old ma," she began. "We always had to sneak out. We couldn't just say, ma we're going to a dance and be honest about it. No we had to lie our way around, saying we're going visiting or going somewhere. This one time we were out after 1 a.m. It wasn't our fault. It was winter and very cold. The cars then were not like cars today. The radiator froze and cracked. We were stuck out there, freezing with no heat. We didn't get back until 3 a.m."

Ma held everyone spellbound as she continued her story, "What to do--How do we get into the house without waking ma? We told the girls before we left that we'd knock on the bedroom windows if there was a problem."

She started to laugh and everyone at the table joined in, even my Grandmother.

"They let us in. I sneaked in first. None of us thought ma would know or even care. If she asked in the morning what time we got in, we'd say midnight."

More fits of laughter erupted. Nonni herself was greatly amused.

"Instead she must've seen the time and realized we were not home and said 'Where the heck are those devils?' As I sneaked in, she was sitting there with a broom ready. But when she saw the look of surprise on our faces, even she had to laugh and couldn't bring herself to holler. 'Okay, I'll fix you in the morning' she said."

Like that wonderful finale to Frank Capra's movie "It's a Wonderful Life," this scene in my grandparent's kitchen unfolded, and has replayed many times in my mind—my grandmother already into her seventies, Mary, 50, Rose and Ella in their early forties, Ziz, Laura and Mimi, in their mid to late thirties, and the baby, V, 32.

It was now nearing time for the evening's highlight—the arrival of Santa Claus. Yes, our family did have their own Mr. Claus thanks to Aunt Ella Russo who had purchased a Santa suit and cast my oldest Cousin Carl (D.O.B. 1920) just back from being shot at on European battlefields to play the role. This was a Santa without reindeer or sleigh, instead opting to tool around town in a coupe with a rumble seat—a hep cat Santa, our own Santa Carl.

So at exactly 11 o'clock, impish Ella went into action. She pranced to the front window, cupping her hand to an ear and with a wild eyed look she asked: "Did anyone hear bells....sleigh bells?" No sooner did she say this there was a stampede to her side and a straining to hear. Naturally, we heard nothing. Nonetheless the seed was planted which of course was what she wanted. It wasn't long before she asked again: "Did anyone hear sleigh bells?"

Not long afterward, Santa Carl made his appearance in the front hall, stomping about, ringing his bell and shouting, "Ho, ho, ho!" He carried a big bag of presents slung over his shoulder.

Once inside, he went into his routine. First came a request for a chair, then a glass of Nonni's prized homemade wine, made with a kick—Santa Carl was always thirsty--though God only knew how he managed wearing a mask. He quickly began doling out gifts in his Santa Carl voice, enunciating each child's name with great care: "Ei-leen, Jer-ome, Paul, Bob-by, Ju-dy. Ma and her sisters acted as Santa Carl's helpers--pulling out gifts from under the tree, holding them up, sometimes shaking them for effect, anything to wet our delirium. A small mountain of wrapping paper and ribbons grew on the floor while the helpers kidded with Santa.

"Oh, Santa, how's the wine? Your cheeks are so red. How about another glass? Someone get Santa another glass," they chirped. Lots of snickering was going on among the helpers. As if that wasn't enough Santa Carl's new bride, Cousin Rita, who until recently was a member of the Cahill clan of women living a few doors up the street, stepped forward and asked, "Oh Santa, may I have a kiss?" With that, she brushed her hand against Carl's mask. The whole room then exploded in laughter. And on and on it went.

Naturally, we kids just didn't get any of these adult shenanigans. Santa Claus was real to us, mask and all. Who else could he be, clearly not our oldest Cousin Carl.

Some years were bigger bonanzas for us than others. On those occasions, ma and the girls pooled their money if a big ticket item was involved such as train sets and movie projectors and the card attached would read "from Santa."

Santa Carl made his getaway out the same doors but in a much more jovial and buoyant state. Someone blocked off the hall and the porch window from view so we could not see where his lovely young reindeers were parked. One last ringing of his bell and a hearty "Ho, ho, ho" not to be seen again in these parts until next Christmas. (*As the years passed and we became more aware, my cousins and I decided he probably had turned right on the porch and slipped through the second floor doorway and made his escape to my Aunt Peggy Sullivan's second floor flat.*)

Figure 5: Christmas at Aunt Ella's, 1950's

Some years we went to Midnight Mass at St. Joseph Cathedral but this Christmas Eve no one ventured out. Big, spicy Italian sausages sandwiched in fresh Moon Bakery Italian bread were now being served. After one bite my mouth was ablaze, still another sent me running to the kitchen sink for as much cold water as I could drink. A side dish to this was fresh provolone cheese, purchased the day before on Hartford's east side, a personal favorite of mine.

Penny ante Poker was kicking off around Nonni's dining room table with piles of pennies, nickels and dimes lying about. Most of my adult relatives played, both men and women. Dad flashed a smile leading me to believe he had a good hand. Usually these games lasted until three or four in the morning. Setback was another favorite.

By now, my sister and I were zonked. Ma took our hands and led us home. As we trudged exhausted up the front steps, we enjoyed our tree lights shimmering in the front room one last time. Once inside, we approached our own tree, now sheltering a pile of presents. One big one had my name written on it allowing my mind to run wild with fantasies.   In the kitchen, a dish of tapioca pudding sat on the table, believed to be Santa's favorite dessert. Ma said it was put there for him when he arrived during the night but that if we didn't get to sleep soon he might not come. We changed into our pajamas and I tumbled into my bed, sis into her crib.

As the hall light expired, after the creaking of the radiator pipes, just once I thought I heard sleigh bells again. I rose from my bed and peeked through the venetian blinds in hopes of a last glimpse of Santa and his sleigh. Instead, to my great chagrin, nothing could be seen in the storm and darkness and all I heard was the sound of snow whistling off my Nonni's rooftop next door. I looked over and tried to tell my sister but she was already fast asleep.

The Cathedral Of St. Joseph School

In the fall of 1945 as World War II winded down, my parents transferred me out of public school to St. Joseph Cathedral School on Asylum Avenue, one mile from home. For the next nine years, I would study there, including one year of high school. This move was probably initiated by my father, who grew up a staunch Catholic schoolboy, attending St. Patrick Grammar School downtown and then St. Thomas Seminary High School on Collins Street, then on the site of the present St. Francis Hospital.

St. Joseph Cathedral School, more affectionately known as St. Joe's, was staffed by Sisters of Mercy supplemented by a few lay teachers like Mrs. M.L. Crosby in fifth grade and Mrs. Bray in third, Sisters Mary Lawrence, Mary Magdalen, Mary Immaculata, Joseph Kathryn, Mary Avelina, Grace Mary, Theodosius, Clarissa, Vernard, and Robert, with Fr. John Shugrue, a parish priest, as principal, or Fr. James Harrison who coached sport's teams. The school also employed the legendary Ed Cosker as the gym teacher and Mr.

Clancy, as one of the janitors, someone known for his noonday slumbers atop a table in the back room and spuds, (or boiled potatoes and eggs), for lunch. We were served milk and graham crackers for five cents at recess by milk ladies Mrs. Angellilo and Mrs. Macken, a woman who lived next to the school and whose husband also worked at St. Joe's.

State of the art for those times, the original home of St. Joe's— beginning in 1879--was a site at the corner of Capitol Ave and Broad Street. The new school which I would attend opened on Asylum Avenue, directly across from Asylum Hill Congregational Church in 1924. This newly completed structure with tiled hallways, contained a large auditorium, library and small gym, but, more impressively a swimming pool, which few schools had.   There was also a nearly life sized statue of Jesus and his Sacred Heart across from the main office.

Over the decades, St. Joe's accumulated an impressive cadre of distinguished graduates—Connecticut Police Commissioner Edward J. Hickey, Hartford Mayor Ann Uccello, congresswoman Barbara Kennelly, theologian Richard McBride, University of Hartford men's basketball coach Jack Phelan, Judge John Daly and surgeon Richard Crombie.

The school on the hill was a three story building. The basement housed the kindergarten, a lunchroom, which was just benches and long tables, girl's and boy's bathrooms and the janitor's boiler room. The first floor, which connected with the main entrance from Asylum Avenue, contained the Principal's and Nurse's Offices, in addition to grades 1-5. There were also two side stairwells, to the east and west, and a central staircase leading up to the second floor and down to the basement. The school Library was located upstairs along with grades 6-8. The backside of the building on Farmington Avenue had a separate entrance for Cathedral High School, grades 9-10. There was a large auditorium with stage and small gym, locker rooms and a swimming pool also in that wing.

St. Joe's was "flanked…by an impressive rectory, its garden abounding with the housekeeper's cats, and the beautiful…"huge gothic cathedral.

Not exclusively a parish school, St. Joes drew from several corners of Hartford and area towns like West Hartford, Granby, Bloomfield, Windsor and East Harford. In the late 1940's, the student body numbered about 1,100 kids, grades K-10.

Kids like us who lived within the parish, came home for lunch. We had an hour to do this, to and fro, allowing about 15-20 minutes each way, not a lot of time to gulp down a meal. Some of the usual menu items included Campbell's chicken noodle, rice, vegetable and tomato soups, tuna fish, grape jelly and cream cheese, bologna, spam and peanut butter sandwiches, plus milk, and maybe a Hostess cupcake. Beginning in third grade, my usual lunchtime route home took me down Sargeant Street with my good buddy, Ed Drydol, leaving him at his house, returning the same way after eating to join up with Ed on the way back.

All in all, we walked four miles a day, including coming and going and lunchtime, a pretty daunting task when you consider our young age in those lower grades. Nevertheless, we did it, over and over again for years, sometimes while running or walking forward, or with your back to an icy winter wind, trying to beat the clock after lunch or in the morning. We were never late. Had we been, the nuns would have chastised us and I dreaded that.

A small minority of students traveled by city bus. Some from the Blue Hills area caught the Palm Street Bus at the corner of Huntington Street and Ashley. One acquaintance named O'Brien boarded a bus daily to Granby from a location on Homestead Avenue.

Our school had a longstanding reputation for academic excellence, strict discipline and indoctrination into the Baltimore Catechism and all things Catholic. Learning was mostly by rote with sister outlining a chapter on the blackboard and the class copying it for memorization later. Corporal punishment was allowed, being hit on the hand with a ruler a favorite attention getter. Gum chewers could expect to see it pressed to their noses; we could also be banished to the coat room for time outs, or as I once did, suffer the humiliation being forced to sit for hours on a stool in front of the class like a dummy. The rubber hose awaited more serious offenders in the principal's office or in the boy's lavatory. The ultimate punishment was expulsion—out into the "darkness beyond" and a public school.

An older alumni of the school once informed me of an incident when he was a student there years before. A popcorn vendor who liked to peddle his wares on Asylum Avenue in front of the school happened by at lunchtime. Seeing this, he and a buddy sneaked off school grounds to buy a bag but were caught by a nun as they returned to the schoolyard and then taken to the Principal's Office.

As soon as they arrived there, they were whisked to the boy's bathroom in the basement where they were ordered to drop their drawers. Father then punished them with the rubber hose. The storyteller never knew who ended up with his treasured popcorn.

In addition, certain nuns had a well-deserved reputation as seriously scary. Srs. Vernard and Robert were two who fell into this category and I tried to avoid them at all costs which at one point became impossible when Vernard started giving me piano lessons in the convent after school.

Still, even in this regimented system, secret "newspapers" were published within classrooms, clandestine sororities formed and met and forbidden profanities were spewed in the schoolyard, for the most part unbeknownst to those in charge. After all, we were not angels nor saints, just kids.

Usually, I brought home good grades in conduct but occasionally I was kept after school for minor infractions and forced to write some mindless exercise on the blackboard or on paper one hundred times, until my hand cramped up.

Our days were very regimented—lined up by height, mornings and after recess, girls in one line, boys the other. Even now these many years later, I can still rattle off names of smaller kids who shared the front of the line with me: Eddie Drydol, Eddie Kotulski, Mike Angellilo, Roger Fortier, Phyllis Stavola, Francis Guinta, Josephine Giarratano.

Once we started marching anywhere, there was no talking. If the principal happened into our classroom, we had a well-rehearsed greeting, standing and chiming: "Good morning/afternoon, Father" in unison. Report cards came out four times a year and Fr.John Shugrue, our principal, appeared to hand them out individually. Not knowing how I was doing, I usually feared the worst—that Father would redress me in front of everyone. It never happened, but I didn't receive any compliments either.

Some kids, especially the girls but not exclusively, liked to await the arrival of the good sisters in the school yard in the morning and vie for their attention asking "Oh Sister, may I carry your bag," as each appeared, repeated over and over until no more opportunities arose.

There were prayers during the day including the Angelus at noontime. It seemed we were always rehearsing for some event at St. Joseph Cathedral adjoining the school—First Confession and Communion, Confirmation, Crowning of the Virgin Mary every May was one of the highlights of our school year:

> Bring flowers of the fairest,
> Bring flowers of the rarest,
> From garden and woodland
> And hillside and vale;
> Our full hearts are swelling,
> Our glad voices telling
> The praise of the loveliest
> Rose of the vale.

It was quite lovely with a young maiden selected each year, dressed in white, a garland of flowers atop her head. As part of the procession, there was a young lad carrying a flower basket and wearing a cummerbund helping out. My friend, Mike Angellilo, got to do it and still remembers it vividly.

May as the month of Mary lived in our hearts. At the urging of the nuns, I can remember creating my own May altar on my bedroom dresser adorned with a small statue of the Blessed Virgin, my scapular, rosary beads and of course fresh flowers, wild or garden variety. Each day in May that was the focal point of my prayers.

We were also expected to attend the 9 AM children's mass at the Cathedral on Sundays with our class where we were closely monitored by our teacher. Our school had a dress code. Boys wore ties with white shirts in the lower grades. I owned a couple of wide ones which my very patient father taught me to tie.

Unlike now, mass then was pre-Vatican Two, done in Latin with an altar set way back and with a priest with his back to us. We tried to follow along in missals which were books containing the prayers, petitions and scripture readings in both Latin and English. We received the Eucharist in our mouths only, at the Communion rail. Communicants were expected to maintain a strict water-only fast beginning at midnight on Saturday night and lasting until after mass on Sunday morning. This, of course, followed a Friday fish day which was the symbol of Catholic culture in the 1940's. By Sunday, it was not unusual, nor any wonder, to see a classmate faint at the Children's mass from this tough regime, many hours in duration.

The theology of it was: it was a mortal sin if you ate meat on Fridays, or if you didn't fast before receiving Communion, or Communion received without Confession, later declared a heresy. And, of course we all knew because the nuns and Baltimore Catechism told us so, a mortal sin was the most grievous sin you could commit, damning the sinner to hell if not repented.

Jeannie and Bobby Morris, older kids who lived on the second floor of the house next to us, also attended St. Joe's, as did four other sisters and brothers before them. So naturally, when I first started school there I walked with them.

There were two well-worn ways of getting to school. At the corner with Homestead bear left to the light at Garden, crossing and proceeding across the railroad tracks. After that, you got to choose one of them. The east end of Sargeant was home to the Veeder Root factory on its north side, with mainly two family and apartment residences on the other end. My pal Ed's house sat across from the main door to Veeder's.

The neighborhood also housed a major distraction for kids—a small store called "Sam's," well known for its varieties of penny candies, in addition to bubble gum together with baseball cards, soda and popsicles. A kid could always count on finding something good like jaw breakers there, for as little as a few cents.

Ashley and Collins Streets, however, were almost exclusively residential, having experienced rapid growth in the Victorian Age and today are listed as a National Historic District. On Ashley, near Garden there was also a drug store with soda fountain and swivel chairs, candy and comic books, but with goodies usually beyond my means. Of course, it never hurt to look, and I did from time to time.

No matter which of these routes I chose, one block further on each of them intersected Huntington Street where I learned to turn south and follow it straight ahead into the schoolyard. Like the others, Huntington had some exceptional houses, too. One I remember fondly was fronted by a cast iron fence and had a small fish pool in its front yard which got my attention as I passed by.

As a young boy growing up in Catholic school, my world was mostly a world of boys, adventures and mischief. The City of

Hartford was our pearl and we roamed far and wide, before and after school and during vacations.

We were always on the lookout for new ways to explore and expand our horizons, whether it was forging new shortcuts—boys loved shortcuts—walking the railroad tracks, taking the bus downtown, or, as we grew older riding our bikes to almost every known baseball diamond and every corner of Hartford and sometimes West Hartford.

Sometimes this meant finding new ways back and forth from school. Coming home, one way was to take Sumner Street which abutted the Hartford Fire Insurance Co. property until reaching the entrance to their parking lot and then slipping by the guard's house undetected, though sometimes not, (in which case he sometimes gave chase and we had to outrun him) and once inside strolling through its beautiful landscape and ball field to the Garden and Collin's Street gate, then heading home. I did this many times without being caught.

Another frequent trespass involved cutting through the parking lot of Veeder Root factory, surrounded by a high wire fence, at the corner of my street. The gate was always open but there was an office near the Homestead Avenue gate and once in a while an employee would emerge yelling and giving chase. There was another gate, always half open, at Garden Street which I could escape through. Like my experience at the Hartford Fire grounds I was never apprehended here either. It wasn't that I was all that fast, but adult pursuers tended to be slow and out of shape and simply gave up after a short time.

More rarely, I took a private road by a small greenhouse off of Huntington Street right through to Sigourney Street, north bound and over the railroad bridge to Homestead, then south three blocks to my street. There were variations to this last route; you could skip the private road and simply turn west on Collins, Ashley or Sargeant Streets and onto Sigourney proceeding the rest of the trip in the same way.

One after school foray with a gang from Homestead Avenue took us all the way west to Woodland Street and the very long way home, probably measuring a couple of miles. Once I even walked a kid named Gregory Osgood, from my class, all the way to his house on Kenyon Street in the west end, a long way from home.

Over the years, I learned to hook up with other boys when my buddies were not in school or in looking for traveling companions on the way to school. For instance, sometimes I joined the Smith family on the way to school. Most were benign excursions but in fourth grade one of these happenings turned into a nightmare. I took a shortcut with some older kids from Huntington to Sigourney Street, through backyards as young boys loved to do. We came to a wooden fence that didn't look challenging at all and I was last to go. My companions were over in a flash. I put my left hand over the top and hooked my finger on barbed wire which to my astonishment ran the length of the top but was nearly invisible from my side. Being complete strangers to me, the other boys were long gone and never looked back. No one else was around. I could not unhook myself as I was standing on tip toes to ease the pressure. I wasn't bleeding much and the pain wasn't that great, but I was alone and in a panic mode. After a while, a man appeared and found me sobbing. He lifted and unhooked me. I ran all the way home. My parents never took me to a doctor but probably should have, since that finger still is slightly crooked, even today.

Later on in my school days, my knowledge of shortcuts saved the day. It was on a day I must have been kept after school because I found myself walking alone after school alongside Asylum Hill Congregational Church, carrying an armload of books, thinking I was alone. Without warning, a boy from my school named Jimmy wearing a WWII army hat and seemingly out of nowhere sucker punched me from behind, knocking me down. He then jumped on top of me and although he was the same size I couldn't get him off. It quickly got hard to breathe. Finally he released his hold and let me up only to stalk me two long blocks down Huntington Street and halfway up Ashley.

God only knows why this boy attacked me. He wasn't even from my end of town and was heading—I later discovered-- in a direction a long way from his home. Plus, I hardly knew him, though I think he was in the same grade.

I thought I'd never get rid of him, stalking me from about one hundred feet behind me at every step. I suddenly remembered a shortcut my friend Eddie had shown me from his backyard a half a block away from where we were. I took a nearby driveway trying to make it look like my own house, and once in the backyard simply disappeared behind the garage and took the alleyway Ed had shown me through several backyards, emerging near the beginning of Sargeant Street and free of my pursuer.

There were several major annual events at St. Joe's. In the fall, the Turkey Raffle was big. We all took raffle ticket books home and went out door to door in our neighborhood. My Aunt and Godmother, Ella who had many social connections, would help out by selling to her friends. So I did well at this.

During Advent, students acted out a Nativity Play. And in March, everyone in the parish community eagerly looked forward to the St. Patrick's Day Kiddie Revue, a variety show which was filled with skits, song and dance. One of the girls in my grade named Peggy Mularkey, a native of Ireland, got to show off her step dancing.

In at least one year in the lower grades, the school ran a bazaar as a fundraiser and I won a cake playing the roulette wheel, an indispensable part of a Catholic school education. I was so proud, not ever having won anything before. Sitting on a dinner plate, this cake was large with white frosting and I was small (I think I was in fourth grade) and had to carry it home, one mile away. Holding the plate with both hands I managed to get all the way to Sargeant Street, three blocks away but then my arms gave out and I dropped it on the sidewalk. I licked some frosting and then continued home, saddened at leaving my prize behind.

Occasionally we were treated to a feature movie in the auditorium. That's where I first viewed *The Fighting Sullivans* with Thomas Mitchell, one of my favorite period pieces. *Song of Bernadette* was another one. However, other times we were subjected to films like the one about Cardinal Mindszenty in Poland and his torture by Russian communists, *Guilty of Treason,* starring Charles Bickford, one which put the fear of communism in us.

Since the fear of nuclear attack was already in the air, we didn't need to hear more about the red peril. But in Catholic school, you heard it a lot. And St. Joe's began having air raid drills where we all marched to the basement or hid under our desks, as was commonplace in the late 1940's and 1950's. One of the nuns actually told us that any time we heard a plane fly over, we needed to bless ourselves and pray, that it could be the end of the world. It got my attention and I did what she suggested.

In the 1940's, there were few days off because of bad weather. Usually, only blizzard like conditions would close school which was true for all schools then, public and private. And there were no school buses, although some out of parish students rode city ones. The vast majority, like me, walked to school, rain or shine.

Walking to school, had its advantages and disadvantages. In winter, there were times after school with snow piled up along Huntington Street when spontaneous heated snowball battle erupted, back and forth from one side to the other. As boys, we enjoyed picking on girls as targets, launching a hail of snowballs. At times, this backfired when the girls happened to be tomboys or older, in which case they could dish it out, too. Or at other times, older boys from the upper grades would make us the targets and then we had our hands full and got our just desserts. Nonetheless, all things considered, it was great fun.

Unlike public schools, St. Joe's had control over most facets of our lives, and snowballing off school grounds was frowned upon. You were expected at all times to live up to the school's code of conduct. I can remember warnings being sent around from the Principal's Office against snowball throwing on the way home, especially on the main thoroughfare to the school—Huntington Street. But being kids we didn't listen and continued merrily on our way, without skipping a beat

Sometimes, it was fun just trying to tramp over the snow hills that the road plows had left along the street playing King of the Royal Mountain, along the way--or who could push who off. Sliding was another favorite pursuit on icy sidewalks. We'd see how far we could go in one attempt, doing this most of the way home when possible. There were still other times when it was so bone chilling and bleak that all we could manage was to zip up, steel yourself, brave the elements and slog along as best possible.

My first day at St. Joe's was no picnic. We arrived early and the schoolyard, which doubled as the church parking lot on Sunday, rapidly filled with kids. I had no sense of these new surroundings and didn't know anyone except for the Morris kids. Bobby Morris took it on himself to keep an eye out for me. But being a very athletic fifth grader and in great demand for games, he was immediately off and running and very distracted. Meanwhile, I drifted into a packed circle of boys and although I no longer recall the exact circumstances, some older kid deliberately knocked me down causing me to tear the knee of my new pants and scrap my leg. Bobby somehow spotted this and quickly put the attacker in his place. One of the nuns also noticed what happened and sent me to the nurse's office where was treated and eventually released sent to class in a very embarrassed state.

My dad's day off from the composition room at the Hartford Times, given in compensation for having to get out a Saturday paper, fell on Wednesdays. WWII had just ended and with it gas rationing, making it possible for him to pick me up with his car after school once a week, along with a carload of my classmates—Mary Claire Burke, Roger Fortier, Freddie Croker, Johnny Mazznicki and Johnny Boy Sullivan. Over time, dad developed an established route, first dropping off Mary Claire on Atwood Street, then swinging over to Freddie's house at the corner of Sargeant and Woodland Streets, next on to Homestead Avenue for the final drop offs.

On the way, we did a lot of horsing around. As Halloween neared, one of us dreamed up the idea that Freddie's house, which was painted a dark brown or black, was haunted. We howled with laughter over this and made what we thought ghostly sounds like "whooo". I laughed so hard, it brought tears to my eyes. This went on for a couple of weeks but we still wouldn't let it go. It didn't matter that his mother was our den mother for Cub Scouts or that we had been inside his house many times; it was haunted and that was that at least until after Halloween.

In those years just after the war, tuition for attending St. Joe's, if you lived within the parish, was free. One reason was nuns and probably priests were mostly a free labor pool, greatly reducing expenses. And secretarial, medical and maintenance staff, lay teachers and others made only very modest salaries.

Second grade passed fairly uneventfully except for a minor incident involving the girl who sat next to me in the front row named Carol. Our teacher, Sister Mary Lawrence, stepped out of the room and closed the door. However briefly that was, this girl managed to write a note to me which said simply, "Will you marry me?" I was still considering this question when Sister returned and ripped the note from my hand. Clearly, as I was to discover in the days that followed, she thought this trivial event a serious infraction and soon, much to my embarrassment and horror, my parent's presence was required at school. Parents then would strongly support a teacher's view and you were almost automatically condemned. But thankfully my dad didn't share sister's view and nothing more was said or done about it after that day. I breathed a sigh of relief and never talked to that girl again.

The highlight of second grade of course was making my First Confession and Communion. This involved many preparations and rehearsals, especially for Confession. ("Bless me Father for I have sinned, it has been (so many) weeks since my last confession and these are my sins...."). When I finally made my First Confession, I accidentally heard some of the outpouring of a girl in the opposite side of the confessional and almost felt I had fallen into serious sin, as we had been trained to believe. But on second thought, I thought it was a stupid rule, let it go, and never was the worse for it.

The only other thing I recalled about that school year was I made great progress in reading and my grades were all A's and B's.

Figure 6: Cousin Maureen, Margie and Eileen Sullivan, circa 1948

From the earliest grades, my dad took a keen interest in seeing that I was a good student. Even though he never had the opportunity to continue his education after high school, he was very smart and had finished first in his class academically at St. Thomas Seminary High School, as had his older brother Jimmy before him. This was no small accomplishment as he had studied Latin, Greek and also a romance language, plus geometry, physics and basics in school. But the Sullivan family was poor and upon graduation he had to go to work full time to help out.

Dad would check my work every night and help me when I needed it. He would quiz me on spelling words and other homework and made sure I was well-prepared for the next school day. Under his supervision, I excelled.

In those early years at St. Joe's the Sisters of Mercy had a great hold on me and like many of my peers I became all on fire for the Lord and Catholicism. I remember joining a parade the kids in my neighborhood were staging and halting our little band, coaxing them to sit under a tree while I preached the gospel according to Dennis to Jews and gentiles alike. During Holy Week in the same time period I would have dreams at night of being present at the crucifixion of Jesus, leaping out of the crowd like Superman at the last minute to save him.

Early on in third grade with Mrs. Bray, perhaps the first day, as we lined up in the schoolyard I met a new classmate, a blond haired boy, new to the school, and short like me, named Edward Drydol who I immediately hit it off with and would spend many hours together with over the next several years. Eddie lived on Sargeant Street in a yellow, two family house and only a couple of blocks from where I lived. Around the same time, we teamed up with a short, pudgy kid, Ed Kotulski, who lived on Liberty Street on the top floor of an Apartment building, forming the three amigos. We were inseparable from day one.

It wasn't long before Eddie's house became my home away from home and his mom, Nellie, my second mom. She was a wonderful woman who worked at Veeder Root but came home for lunch so she could feed Eddie and his sister, Theresa.

We spent many happy hours in the Drydol's backyard playing stickball, cowboys and Indians, war, cars and trading comic books. Sometimes we joined a classmate, Bobby Monroe, half a block away to play behind his apartment building, on the railroad tracks which in those years were in active use. We quickly became used to playing around the tracks and walking them.

Since St. Joe's strongly urged weekly Confession, the three of us used to trek up to the Cathedral on Saturdays to unburden our souls. Mrs. Drydol would be sure to remind us, as she was always looking out for our spiritual well-being. Besides, the nuns had made us into true believers and we knew our Baltimore Catechism inside out.

One Saturday, following Confession, the devil got to us, in the person of our buddy Eddie Kotulski. Somehow he had heard— maybe through his older brother-- there was a hole in the girl's locker room window and we could get a peek at them naked when they were getting ready to shower, a naughty scheme, indeed. To see if this was true, we sneaked into the garden in back of the rectory and hid behind part of the school ground's wall. We could hear but not see them. Disappointed, we slipped carefully out of the garden of temptation again without being seen and even thought of returning to Confession a, second time to own up to our sin of the flesh. But, Confession had already ended.

Then, along came Mike, or Michael J. Angellilo of Edgewood Street, who became our fourth and final amigo, greatly adding to the stickball action and overall fun.

Fourth grade was pretty uneventful except that my teacher confiscated a glow in the dark ring I had brought to school. It was a cereal box prize that you sent away for in the mail. Of course getting mail of any kind for a nine year old was a big deal and I could not constrain myself when it arrived. Immediately, I hid myself in my bedroom closet to relish the green glow of my acquisition. My big mistake was bringing it to school the next day to show it off. I arrived in the school yard early and passed it around.   All went well until we lined up for class and the nun grabbed the ring from a friend, put in her desk later, and I never got it back. I was heartbroken.

That same year (1948-49), I started piano lessons with Sister Vernard in St. Joseph Convent, next to the Cathedral. To do this, I had to meet her after school at the gate to the Convent grounds and carried her black briefcase for her up to the Music Room on the second floor. I dreaded these meetings as sister had a frightening reputation. In addition, I hated taking piano and wanted to be out footloose and fancy free playing. Moreover, I hardly practiced which didn't help matters. But my mother insisted.

I still remember the nuns had a system of bell ringing to communicate. The number of times a bell rang signaled which nun was being summoned. Every time one rang, we'd halt our lesson while sister listened intently. Once in a while she heard her's and she'd disappear.

The year proceeded along these lines until Easter time when it was announced there was going to be a Passion Play at the Bushnell Memorial on the day of my next lesson. I decided to skip piano and go to the Bushnell instead, all without telling sister. A large group of us from St. Joe's walked to the Bushnell and then home. The next day I was called out of my classroom and told Sr. Vernard wanted to see me in her sixth grade room on the top floor. When I arrived, she demanded her two dollars for the missed lesson and scolded me for my behavior.

Not knowing what to do, I told my father that same night. He became outraged over her demand and there is nothing like an Irishman who is outraged. The next day he came to St. Joe's, yanked me from my class and escorted me to Sister Vernard's sixth grade room. My dad confronted her in the hall and in front of me. "Here's your two dollars," he sneered and continued "And my son will not be taking piano lessons with you anymore." We then stormed off. Needless to say, Sr. Vernard never gave me any trouble again during my remaining several years at the school.

In the springtime of fifth grade, my beloved Father Frank Vincent Sullivan, died of heart disease in St. Francis Hospital. He was 41 years old. I was ten years old and in 5th grade, my sister Eileen was seven.

During Advent, he had suffered excruciating leg cramps at home. One night I recall seeing daddy cry, something I had never seen before. He tried to ease the pain with belts of whiskey but nothing seemed to work. Ma wanted him to go to the hospital which he resisted. In the end, he took me aside and told me he didn't want to but he had to go.

Several years before while undergoing a physical exam, a doctor had disapproved daddy for war related work because his arteries were already so blocked from smoking. Forewarned, he never gave up cigarettes, and even being from a family with a history of serious heart problems brought no change in his behavior. His mother, Abbey, had dropped dead of a massive heart attack on

Homestead Avenue, both his sister, Peggy, and brother Jimmy would succumb to strokes. Only grandpa Michael would escape the scourge, dying of a bleeding ulcer.

Still, for a short while at least, life seemed to go on like normal. We made frequent visits to the hospital and it seemed to me that he was holding his own. I even remember bringing him my report card to see because I knew it would please him. I had all A's and B's that term, one of my best.

Nearing springtime, daddy seemed to be improving mightily and there was talk, however briefly, of him coming home at last. I was so excited by this possibility. Little did I know that sometimes patients perked up just before they died. Two days later, he took a turn for the worse.

They rushed me to his bedside. He was in and out and in a very weakened state. He criticized my mother for bringing me saying, "I told you not to bring him. I didn't want him to see me like this."

At one point, he drifted off and when he came back claimed he had seen his parents and siblings in a beautiful dream. Before we left, he made my aunt Ella Russo, my godmother, promise to watch out for me.

I left feeling sick. The next day the doctor came and announced I had the measles. As it turned out, so did my sister. At the time of his death, I was bedridden along with Eileen. Consequently, neither of us attended his funeral.

The night of his death my Nonni Lorenzo entered our darkened bedroom and cried out "O dio, your daddy's gone. You're the man in the family now." *What is she talking about? I just saw daddy. He's alright. He's coming home soon.* She scared me. I started having second thoughts about the situation, so much so that I reached for my rosary beads and began praying feverishly. However, no one else told me anything.

Measles were followed not long after by the mumps which only delayed anyone telling us daddy's fate. In the day's that followed my tomboy friend, Tootsie DeLucco, who lived up the street, stopped by my bedside and presented me with a brand new baseball which lifted my spirit.

It wasn't until we were both fully recovered from our illnesses that ma finally sat us down and told us of his passing. I was so upset I couldn't even cry. Daddy was my rock. He had saved my life at the Circus Fire, guided my development, assisted my learning, took me everywhere with him. It would be many years before I came to terms with his loss. I missed him terribly. As for ma, she became a nervous wreck. There was no help in dealing with our grief, or probably not ma's either, and I never felt comfortable talking to her about it. Life went on but I was now an angry young boy.

Later I was informed that St. Joseph Cathedral was filled for my dad's funeral mass and that men from the Garden Tavern and Restaurant where daddy tended bar part time had taken up a collection and had come to our door with a stash of money to help defray funeral expenses. Well-known Hartford Times Sport's writer, Art McGinley, mentioned my father in his column saying about how strange it seemed not to have him around.

Returning to school when I got better was hard. It weighed on me that I was now somehow different from the other kids, now being fatherless. But I kept it all inside.

As I progressed at St. Joe's, the schoolyard, gym and recess became more and more fun. A couple of my favorite outdoor games were ring-a-levio and leap frog. We also used a strip of earth near the schoolyard fence to play marbles. And in winter, we sometimes were treated to large mounds of snow from the plows used to clear the yard which doubled as a church parking lot on Sundays. On those days, we used up all our recess time sliding down these miniature mountains. I think the nuns were envious of our fun.

Gym class was outdoors in good weather, basically fall and spring, and in the gym the rest of the time. We exercised and played basketball, kick ball and softball. Occasionally, we had swimming which I never mastered. When we played softball, Mr. Cosker, our gym teacher, would give a boy money to get him a milk shake at Arthur Drugs, a block or so away. I never was chosen but didn't care. Who wanted to miss a good softball game?

I also became familiar with profanity by hearing words mouthed in the schoolyard and sometimes political slogans as in the heat of the 1948 presidential campaign:

> *Truman, Truman, rah, rah, rah,*
> *Dewey, Dewey,*
> *Throw him in the ash can,*
> *Hah, hah, hah.*

That Lenten season our class was studying Christ's entry into Jerusalem riding on an ass, the Gospel according to Mark. One of my classmates had just read this aloud and two boys and I began to snicker over use of the word ass. Sister Clarissa wheeled around and saw what was happening. The other suspects managed to suppress their expression but I got caught smirking. The nun castigated me in front of the class and then made me take a seat on a stool in front of everyone for the next two hours. It was probably my worst moments at St. Joe's—Dennis, as the Dunce.

This same woman could be scary at times. When she got really upset with us her favorite tactic was to lift the top of one of our heavy wood desks and slam it down with all her might. The poor sister's hands would then shake violently. In retrospect, I think she may have suffered from high blood pressure. But, her dramatic gestures certainly got our attention.

Once, when she was writing on the blackboard with her back turned away from us, two boys rose and started duking it out. I can still play it back in my mind like a slow motion sequence in a movie; it was such an unusual happening. One culprit's name was Roger. The two of them were sent to the office and expelled, never to be seen again. I never found out whether they got a rubber hosing for a goodbye. In my eight years at St. Joe's, it was the only time I ever saw anyone ever fight in class, apparently another unforgivable sin.

That same year, I was introduced to the world of Catholic school making out. A boy in my class named Donny threw a birthday party at his house over near Frog Hollow. To get there, I caught a ride with Bobby Higgins and his older brother plus Roger Fortier, another classmate. The party was all about Spin the Bottle and Post Office, beginning to end, nothing else—all the parties were in those years. I can't even remember if there was a cake I was so distracted.

So many kids from school were there that many had to sit on the living room floor awaiting their turns out in the hallway. We got to kiss some of our cutest classmates and then some not so cute.

When I turned twelve, the good sisters made us all take an oath that we would not drink alcoholic beverages until our twenty first birthday. Within a few weeks, we were invited to Sunday dinner at my Nonni's house right next door. As food was being served, my grandmother's homemade wine was also parceled out to everyone. Some was poured in my glass but I protested explaining about the oath I had taken at school. Hearing this, my grandmother immediately countermanded the order, commenting in broken English: "It putta da color in your cheeks."

From then on, I drank wine with my meals at Nonni's table, laced with a little ginger ale, her home brewed wine being considered too strong for growing boys.

My final two years there I was lucky enough to be in the same class as a girl named Marilyn who loved to party on her birthdays, at least I think that was the occasions. She lived several blocks from me on Homestead Avenue in an apartment building. In seventh grade, she threw her first one around Halloween time in her cellar. We started out innocently enough bobbing for apples. But, as the night moved forward, Spin the Bottle took over and girls were lining up outside coal bins to kiss the boys of their dreams especially one named Bobby with the curly hair.

Later, someone suggested playing Flashlight, for which all the lights were soon switched off. Just as everyone was jostling in the darkness, the cellar door popped open and a shaft of light broke through. It was someone's mom yelling "Beatrice," her daughter's name, from the top of the stairs. Panic reigned for a moment with kids breaking apart and a very embarrassed girl leaving the scene with her mother.

The following year Marilyn had moved about half a block further up Homestead and now had a paneled recreation room in her cellar, the first I had even seen. I think she invited everyone in Sister Avelina's classroom, which I was again lucky enough to have been in. I can still see it—the girl's seated on one side, the boy's on the other. Some of the eighth grades best looking Catholic girls were in attendance, eagerly awaiting their turns. The appointed kissing location was under the stairs, there being no coal bin available at her newest residence. There were many flushed faces and erections that night. Had they known, the good sisters would have been mortified and the confessional would have been in order.

Gradually during that school year, I became friends with a kid in my class named Billy, who introduced me to some new adventures. He lived in a nearby apartment house and we went there after school one day and sampled some of his parent's whiskey using shot glasses. On Friday nights, we attended movies at West Middle School on Asylum Avenue, on the prowl for girls but were never successful. We also started acting up in class and having to sometimes stay after school as punishment. Still, looking back at my report card it didn't seem to impact my academics that much....not yet at least.

I remember the spring of 1952 as one of the most beautiful of my life; lots of sunny days and few bad ones. Filled with the growing exuberance of being young, I'd bounce up Homestead Avenue mornings heading for school singing "Zippity doo dah" or "Oh What a Beautiful Morning." Coming home in the afternoon, I'd pluck roses off the front fence of Veeder Root's Factory for the fun of it.

And, as I progressed in age and grade, I started to ride my bike to and from school, lots of times carrying Ed Drydol with me on my crossbar. This took place on fair weather days, especially in spring when Asylum Hill could be very beautiful. At other times, Ed and I honed our baseball skills playing catch with a rubber or tennis ball up and down Huntington Street, running right out into the road—there being a lot less car traffic in those years.

Granted, these scenes seem idyllic all these years later but it really was like that—a wonderful time of innocence in childhood and in society. We could spend most of the day at the park with friends and no one worried about us. We could catch a bus downtown alone or with friends without any adults. Most likely, your biggest threat if you were a boy came from other boys who turned into bullies. It seemed many neighborhoods had at least one.

One hundred and twelve girls and boys graduated from eighth grade at St. Joe's that year, all of us decked out in white, and all of us posing for a group photo in front of St. Joseph Cathedral Rectory on Farmington Avenue with Fr. John John Shugrue, our principal, looking every bit the innocents we were. I was seated on the grass with the shorter boys. The world awaited us.

Figure 7: 51 - 53 Irving St.

51 – 53

As I mentioned earlier, all of my grandparents lived under the same roof at 51-53 Irving Street, the Lorenzos being the landlords on the first floor, the Sullivans, the renters upstairs. This arrangement began in the early 1930's. Over a decade later in 1943, we moved next door to them.

However, my Father's mother, Abbie died in July of 1933, long before I was born, walking home from a novena at St. Ann's Church on Park Street. According to newspaper accounts, she suffered a massive heart attack on Homestead Avenue around the corner from Irving Street.

Relatives have told me she was a tall, red head, who favored long dark dresses. Born into a large farm family, coincidentally named Sullivan, in Castle Cove on the Ring of Kerry, she married my grandfather in Ireland and immigrated here with him in 1901, making landfall in New York on St. Joseph Day, March 19. Her ancestors had been Galvins and Sullivans, his Sullivans mixed with Butlers. Judging from the circumstances of her death, it is fairly safe to say she was a pious person and from her background that she spoke with a brogue. The fact that she lost at least three children during childhood may qualify her as a woman of sorrow.

Michael, my Irish grandfather, was a quiet man who enjoyed his pipe and an occasional pint of ale with his sons at the Garden Grill or Golden Oak Tavern on Albany Avenue. Grandpa came from Beenbane, a subsection of Waterville, home to the Transatlantic Cable Station and later Charlie Chaplin during his summer hiatuses, on the Ring of Kerry.

Like my Italian grandfather, Michael found employment for the City of Hartford as a laborer, Grandpa Sullivan in the Water Department, my Dadone in the Street Department. Even for those times, he was a short man, measuring about five feet five. One of my strongest memories of him growing up was discovering he had false teeth and that he kept them in a jar next to his bed when not in use. My sister, cousins and I used to sneak into his room to get a peek at them. Aside from my memory of his teeth, my most vivid other remembrance of Michael was of him sitting on the front second floor porch smoking his pipe and reaching into his small change purse to parcel out pennies to me as a small boy. He died of a bleeding ulcer in November of 1946 when I was turning eight.

He was literate, nevertheless, he labored for many years at humble City of Hartford jobs which guaranteed years at poverty level wages and resultant living conditions on the Avon and Kennedy Streets for his family.

Typical wages at this level: fifty cents an hour for a forty eight hour work week. It wouldn't be until their three children completed high school in the late 1920's and entered the work force that the Sullivans could finally afford to move on up out of the eastside onto Irving Street in the more prosperous north end.

The other grandfather, Dominic Lorenzo, stood five feet eight, with bushy eyebrows not unlike my own and a moustache that looked like one of the brooms he pushed on city streets for his job. His hair was brown, cropped short and greying as he aged. Dadone was lean and fit from years of hard, physical labor. He did not speak English and was illiterate like my grandmother.

His boyhood home was Matrice, in the Province of Campobasso, Italy, where he was the second born in a family of stone masons. Descended from marriages of Laurienzos and Gambatesas, and before that Reales, Spinellis, Daddarios, DeVitos, Coloccias and Colavitas. Dadone (*Da-down*), as we called him, came from a family of six boys and one girl.

When he reached manhood, he and some of his brothers, immigrated to Brazil where he met and married my Nonni. Some believe there were strange circumstances surrounding the Lorenzo boys departure from Italy. One family story alleges they fled the old country because of a blood feud with a neighboring clan.

There is no proof of this, however. As for his new life in Brazil, the only information that's been handed down was that Dadone and one of his brothers hired out as musicians on the local café scene, my grandfather on the concertina and his brother, guitar.

Dadone was a very quiet man. Whether this was due to stoicism because of his lowly position in life, or that this was his natural inclination, I can't say. When I was a boy, he had one known pleasure: smoking his pipe, which sadly was restricted by my grandmother's ruling that he could not do this inside the house. I also remember he owned a spittoon which he stored in the kitchen. On very rare occasions, Dadone got out his concertina and played. Once, he performed magic tricks for his daughters.

Unfortunately, his inability to speak English made it difficult to get a fix on him. What was obvious: my grandmother had him tamed and at her beck and call. She always had her projects for him, especially once he was retired. He was part of her labor pool, along with my uncles, who maintained her properties pro bono.

He also enjoyed finding time away from my grandmother. One of his favorite escapes was a cot he kept on the ground floor of their Portland Street property where he sometimes hid out. On at least one of these occasions, he was joined by my first cousin Paul Ostiguy, then a boy. At some point, my cousin noticed a mirror Dadone kept angled in such a way in the front window so that he could keep an eye out on the street in case my grandmother was approaching. My cousin thought this ingenious. When she finally did approach, he looked over at Paul with his finger to his lips: "S-h-h!," he pleaded, tilting the blinds closed. Paul never forgot that day.

At still other times, he combined work and escape by hiking to their East Hartford property, not far from the Connecticut River, where they grew a vegetable garden and where he kept another cot in a hut.

As a boy, I once made this same trip with him. His goal on that hot summer day was to pick up a lengthy piece of pipe and haul it back to Irving Street, miles away, which he did. It was the kind of brute labor he spent his life doing. Even when well up in years, my grandmother always seemed to have projects for him. There would be no respite for Dominic.

The only other information concerning him came from my mother, late in her own life. She told me that Dadone had thrown her across her bedroom in a rage, when she was growing up. In my mind, such an act seemed totally out of character for the man I remember, so quiet and meek. Yet, my mother insisted it was true and wouldn't let it go.

Figure 8: Nonni

My Italian grandmother Lillian was the grandparent I remember the most. We called her Nonni, the short form of Nonnina, an endearing term like granny or gramma. Born Libretta, however like other newcomers to America looking for acceptance in the early 20th century, she changed her name to the more anglicized, Lillian. Barely standing five feet tall, she was totally illiterate and signed with an X her whole life. She descended from a line of DeStephanis on her father's side, Presutti's, Giovannucci's, on her mother's.

After studying closely the earliest known photo of her taken with her entire family in front of 53 Irving Street in 1933 when she was nearly sixty years old, I have come to conclude she must have been attractive as a young woman, pretty even. In it, her facial features project very pleasant qualities, especially her captivating eyes. Prior to this reevaluation, I never felt that way, perhaps because I only knew her later when she had aged considerably, or perhaps because she had built a reputation as being cold and nasty.

Early in her childhood years—most likely in the 1880's—her parents Maria and John DeStefano immigrated from Italy to Ribeiras, Pito, near Sao Paolo, Brazil, where they came to own a small coffee plantation. There, my grandmother grew up in a wild west kind of environment, at least according to some of the stories she handed down.

During that decade it's clear they must have achieved some measure of prosperity because they ended up owning land, slaves and at least one horse of their own.

At a young age, she learned to ride horseback which was probably a necessity of life in those days. But, more than that, I believe she came to enjoy riding evidenced by the fact that when she made the voyage to American in 1906 she brought her riding britches with her through steerage.

The return to riding never materialized once here. Her britches would stay packed away in a chest, first in eastside tenements and then in the cellar of her own house on Irving Street, until her grandchildren discovered them half a century later, long after the age of horse transportation had ceased. I remember holding them and wondering what stories they held.

In the Brazilian countryside, another real necessity of life was owning and knowing how to use a gun. Nonni said almost every household had one. One of her stories from this time in her life involved a time she was outside atop the family woodpile pulling pieces but was shocked to find it moving from underneath. Investigation showed there was a boa constrictor situated there and was moving about. She screamed and her mother came running with her gun and promptly shot the snake dead, eventually giving the carcass to the family slaves. Still another hand me down bit of family lore had one of her brothers being killed in a bar room shootout locally.

Her parents owned at least two slaves-- a man and woman. Slavery as an institution was not outlawed in Brazil until later in the decade of the 1880's. In her later years, she reminisced about an incident from her childhood involving her father and a slave who was giving him trouble. Like a scene from the Bible, her father drew a cross in the dirt using a stick, looked the man in the eye saying "Do not disrespect me or you will end up here."

The only other story from her life in Brazil was that of her father's death. John had been out riding during a storm when he was thrown from his mount into a ditch and knocked unconscious. He wasn't found until the following day but by that time he had been exposed to the elements too long and died a few days later.

His tragic ending sent the family reeling. Maria DeStefano, Nonni's mother started drinking heavily. It became difficult to make ends meet. No one will ever know for sure now the exact details, but with the death of John, their financial situation worsened and would never be the same.

Sometime in this time period my grandmother met and married my grandfather Dominic Lorenzo. By today's standards, they were both very young, 18-22 years old. They wasted no time in starting a family. After the loss of one child, my grandmother gave birth to Brasilia (aka Mary) in 1897.

The family financial situation deteriorated still further. Maria's drinking continued and she decided to return to Italy. There, she lived out her days with a strict brother-in-law who beat her because of her alcoholism.

Meanwhile, my grandparents, with four young children in tow, plus a brother of Nonni's, his wife and baby, managed to scrape enough money together to board the liner Byron and immigrate to the United States, making landfall in New York harbor in April, 1906. They made the trip to Hartford by riverboat and settled in a tenement at 17 Front Street, down by the Connecticut River where many first generation Italians lived.

In all probability, they froze in winter with no central heat and roasted in summer. Many of these buildings still had outhouses. Later they would move to 474 Front Street (about where Constitution Plaza one day would be), which at that time was unpaved. There were also several house of ill fame on the eastside.

Brasilia (aka Mary), Adelaide, Pauline (aka Rose) and Erminia (aka Ella), who was an infant, came with them on the ship. Everyone except for Adelaide, who was about six years old, made it through

Ellis Island. She was denied entry because she had a sty on her eye, along with Nonni's brother and his wife and their baby who was sick. They were summarily deported back to their original port of departure which was in Italy, though in Adelaide's case it was probably fortunate that it wasn't Brazil. There she would have been alone. At least in Italy, she had relatives. Once in Italy relatives took her in until she was old enough to reapply for immigration to the U.S. Unfortunately for her, American law required that she wait until she was sixteen years old.

In the summer of 1911, the great heatwave hit Front Street, quickly making life nearly unbearable. With their tin roofs, tenements turned to ovens. According to news reports, horses and people dropped dead in their tracks from the heat and some driven to despair committed suicide. A local man went crazy downtown climbing a telephone pole and had to be subdued with a straight jacket. In the poor sections of Hartford like Front Street, babies were dying. Women walked the streets holding their little ones, moaning and crying. My grandmother with five young children, and most importantly Claudia (aka Laura) who was an infant had to be very anxious. For all we know, she may have been one of the mothers walking the eastside cradling her baby girl.

It took the Lorenzos two decades to climb out of poverty. They did this with my grandmother at the reins. From those earliest times, she ran a matriarchy, where men in the family had little say. This little woman gave the orders, others, especially my grandfather and sons-in-laws simply obeyed and followed.

The Lorenzo daughters were sent out to work as early as possible. Much to my mother's regret, being second oldest, she was yanked out of St. Patrick School in seventh grade to go to work in local tobacco sheds and sweat shops. This was the usual fate of the oldest Lorenzo girls. The more fortunate younger ones got to work in a factory like Colt's or at Veeder-Root's.

By the 1920's, ma had already logged ten years of work experience, her latest employ being a factory at Wiley, Bickford & Sweet, located at 80 Pliny Street. At that same time, her sister Ann was working close by at 53 Pliny Street and Ella was at Colt's Manufacturing.

Ma's younger sister, Aunt Ann (aka Yolanda) once told me how the system worked. On a typical payday, Nonni set up shop at the kitchen table, waiting to collect the salary of each daughter as they arrived home.

There was no allowance or spending money for them. Since it was cash, Aunt Ann said she learned to pilfer a little money for herself before showing up at home which was the best she could do.

With this bonanza, my grandmother began buying properties. The first purchase was the multi-family tenement at 53 Portland Street where they also moved. Soon, she began collecting her first rent money, which she made her own personal vocation.

Her time on the eastside was not without incident. Portland, Avon and Pleasant Streets, known as part of the Windsor District, also housed "disorderly houses," or houses of prostitution, and objects of raids by the vice squad. One place was right across the street from my grandparent's home. In the fall of 1926, Nonni got into a fight with her next door neighbor, a Mrs. Kaplan. According to the Hartford Courant my grandmother had spread the word that Kaplan was a stool pigeon for the police and had supplied information leading to the latest raid.

It's hard to say why Nonni, referred to as "Lily" in the newspaper, didn't like her neighbor's action. On the contrary, one would have thought she would have applauded Mrs. Kaplan. However, one complicating factor may have been the fact that her own brother had been spotted frequenting a house nearby and my grandmother was fuming about this sighting, a source of embarrassment to her. What if he had been swept up in the raid? Would she still have vented her wrath on Mrs. Kaplan?

Over the years, she purchased two family houses on Irving Street (circa 1930 and 1940), Webster Street (circa 1929), Maplewood Avenue, West Hartford (circa mid 1940's), plus a cottage at Giant's Neck Beach in the early 1950's.

Nonni was Nonni, a thoroughly old country Italian and woman of the soil. She spoke little English but loved to gab with family in Italian. St. Anthony's Church, with its mass in Italian, was her church of choice. Oh how I detested accompanying her there, since I couldn't understand a word they were saying. She said the rosary in Italian, sometimes with her youngest granddaughter, Donna. I remember her being able to dramatically act out at wakes, moaning "Oh, dia, oh dia," and dropping to her knees for affect. One of her favorite dishes was simply dunking pieces of Italian bread in a bowl of olive oil and tomatoes and asking everyone at the table to join in with, "Manga." She grew grapes for her homemade wine at her Webster Street property in the south end and produced the most wonderful fresh pasta in a special cellar room.

In addition to a well-manicured lawn and a yard awash in roses along the wire fence that separated our yards and hybrid yellow ones in the backyard, she kept hydrangea bushes near her front steps and Iris flowers and a peach and cherry tree out back. At the very back of her yard, she had a vegetable garden that yielded annual harvests of tomatoes, beans, peppers and parsley, regardless of the rats that were always burrowing.

She even had her own home remedy for not being able to sleep: dunk Italian bread in milk, preferably after midnight.

In the early 1960's when I was still in college, Nonni came to suspect my unsuspecting French Canadian uncle Armand, whose young family lived with her, of planning to steal some of her money from her. Our phone rang and I listened intently as she implored me to come and see her, the first and last time she ever called for me. "Danny, (Denny in her heavy Italian accent always translated as Danny) come to my house. I need you."

Fearing a medical emergency, I rushed over. Instead, I was shocked to find her with a large, open chest filled with money sitting on her bed. She asked me to count it, which I did. It was the most money I've ever seen in one place, certainly the most cash I ever handled. In it were bills from the past that were unlike any I knew. After the accounting, I left feeling she was satisfied that nothing was amiss.

Nevertheless, it didn't end there. In the days to follow, I learned that two of my uncles, Sam and Joe, were urgently summoned as *fixers*, their mission to construct a false ceiling in her closet to hide her chest full of money. They built one according to plan and then placed the chest inside. They put a final touch to their work adding a mouse trap, just in case any thieving fingers reached up there. None ever did. But she strongly suspected my uncle who lived with her.

This situation may have represented my grandmother's worst hour since everyone knew my uncle was honest to a fault. He'd be the last person you'd catch stealing, especially from this his mother-in-law. Yet this was the declining state of my grandmother's mind as she approached ninety years old.

Not long after this, her daughters convinced her that our neighborhood had grown too dangerous a place to be hiding her savings in. *Ma, someone will kill you for that much money, they cautioned.* She accepted their counsel and promptly deposited her stash in the Society of Savings Branch Bank at the corner of Blue Hills and Albany Avenues. Incredibly, she made the deposit at face value, not giving any thought to the possible added worth of the collectible currency she owned. All her frugality and shrewdness amounted to little in the end. We always wondered what happened to those rare bills.

Nonni did not believe in paying out to maintain her properties, the exception being for work her sons-in-law, my grandfather, or she, couldn't handle which wasn't often. An exception was her brother, Ralph, who got the nod for any tree work, as he was an arborist for the City. Case in point, the three bedroom cottage she had built at Giant's Neck Beach in the early 1950's by John Sylvester, the former husband of a family friend who was a local builder. Once built, it became her pride and joy where she could offer relatives weekends--and sometimes, weeks—at the shore but only if you came to work. My mother and her sisters showed up to do housework, cooking and gardening, especially the latter. Their husbands, my uncles, were called upon for all kinds of manual labor: an enclosed front porch and a large family room were two of their projects. Nor were Kids completely excused from the workload. At one point in the cottage's infancy, large boulders had to be extracted from the soil in order to properly landscape the front yard. To get the job done, we had to dig down three or four feet with pick, shovel, and crow bar removing smaller stones first to get at the big ones. It was tough, sweaty work which my uncles did the brunt of, but we did help out. Next, we had to figure out how to remove ones too heavy to lift. My uncles solved this engineering problem by attaching a chain from the back of one of their cars to the rock in question and then driving it across the road and into the woods.

Even in his declining years, Dadone was not exempted from the Lorenzo labor machine and my grandmother always seemed to have a project. I can still see them in their seventies, moving one of our four foot wide flagstone sidewalks slabs that had worked its way loose, using a pick, shovel and crowbar and then putting it back in place, taking constant breathers. Or there is the vision of my grandmother, well into her eighties, up on a ladder propped against her house and pounding away with a hammer.

It was her nature to be combative. As a young boy, Cousin Bobby Ostiguy accompanied her on a shopping trip to see the "chicken man" downtown. While examining the chickens for sale, holding them upside down, she noticed their beaks had been stuffed with paper to disguise the fact that this particular batch had been sickly creatures. Her outrage vented against the shopkeeper haunted young Robert from that day onward.

A continual state of animosity existed between Lillian and her Italian neighbors and fences were erected between yards. The wounds never seemed to heal and an uneasy peace existed.

Seemingly fearless, she waged war against the monster rats that invaded our yard at the time of downtown urban renewal. Almost overnight it seemed these rodents, some the size of cats, had nested in an open area under the back of our house. Well into her eighties, there she was squatting under there pouring rat poison down their holes. *Ma, what're you doing there, her daughters cautioned? But she never listened.*

On another warm summer day in the mid 1960's, and again when she was well up into her eighties, she was enjoying some time in her rocker on the front porch, leaning forward on her cane. Diagonally across the way, a newcomer to the street came out of her house to recline herself on a chaise lounge accompanied by her brood of young children. Although new to the area, this woman had already established herself in local consciousness as badly overweight and bizarre, preferring to parade around in bikini type bathing suits, both on the block and even braving the catcalls she attracted on Albany Avenue.

This day started quietly enough for her except that at some point paranoia suddenly seized her and she imagined my grandmother, who was simply soaking up the local scene, to be a threat. Gathering up all her little ones, she came charging across the street directly at my grandmother. Nonni rose gripping her cane and started down the stairs.

Mrs. Sylvester, our upstairs neighbor, noticed this unfolding from her window and rushed down to join the fray.

The women were already grappling when she arrived, my Nonni yelling "fongool." Mrs. Sylvester tried to get a grip on the woman's hair only to discover it was a wig and it came off. By this time, the police had been called. The woman was taken away in the cruiser and the State of Connecticut took control of her children. We never saw her again.

The episode was classic Lillian.

"Blessed are they that mourn, for they shall be comforted." St. Matt. V. 5.

My Jesus have mercy on the Soul of

Abbie J. Sullivan
Died July 26, 1933
Age 54 years

PRAYER

O GENTLEST Heart of Jesus, ever present in the Blessed Sacrament, ever consumed with burning love for the poor captive souls in Purgatory have mercy on the soul of Thy departed servant.

Abbie

Be not severe in Thy judgment but let some drops of Thy Precious Blood fall upon the devouring flames, and do Thou O merciful Saviour send Thy angels to conduct her to a place of refreshment, light and peace. Amen.

May the souls of all the faithful departed through the mercy of God, rest in peace. Amen.

Eternal rest grant unto her, O Lord! and let perpetual light shine upon her. Sacred Heart of Jesus, have mercy on her. Immaculate Heart of Mary, pray for her. St. Joseph, friend of the Sacred Heart pray for her.

(100 days for each aspiration)

Figure 9:

Child of the Times

Figure 10: Jerome Montano, Hertzel Rotenstein, Jackie Krefak

Front row: Henrietta Solomon, Eileen Sullivan (late 1940's)

Our neighborhood was the melting pot—Christians and Jews, Italian, Polish, Irish, French, Ukralnian, Greek, Jamaican, and a Connecticut Yankee, living side by side, not always harmoniously but at least most of the time—Dominick DeLucco, the future mayor and restaurateur; Jenny Cohen, the bakery worker; Joe Solomon, shop owner in downtown; Charles Morris, the factory worker; George Stylle, owner of Wonder Diner on Albany Avenue; Guy Aiello, the fireman; Danny Ermakovich, the mailman and his brother Johnny, the grease monkey; Charlie Schlicker, the salesman; Rose Yush, the school secretary and war widow; Max Rotenstein, Beatrice Auerbach's accountant; Jessie Maule, the dressmaker; Harold Larensen, factory worker, and my father, Frank Sullivan, the linotype operator for the Hartford Times.

Most neighbors knew each other at least by sight, if not to talk to. It was a world of surrogate parents, especially mothers. They knew whose kids were whose and looked out for us. Not always but some of the time, families welcomed us onto their porches, yards and into homes. Notable among them: the Johnsons, Yush-Cohens and Rotensteins. On the other hand, it could be a virtual minefield, given the presence of biddies, like Mrs. Phillips living across the street from us, and others, like my own grandmother, who did not take kindly to children.

At times the neighborhood peace was broken by turf wars. For instance, my grandmother never got along with Patsy Pietro, who lived next door, or Mr. Zito in the house behind her on Magnolia Street. They argued over petty things. This led Pietro to erect a chain link fence between our yards. At the edge of my grandparent's backyard, old man Zito had a long wooden fence separating his from Nonni's.

These conflicts hardly ever affected neighborhood kids growing up. Rather, we went about our merry way.

Lots of times, the street itself acted as our playground. In good weather, we rode bikes, played baseball, softball, kick ball, football, and hopscotch. We also jumped rope and roller skated on the sidewalks up and down the street and around the block until day's end, or until someone filed a complaint with the Hartford Police. At the sight of a cruiser, we'd high tail it to someone's backyard to hide. Once in a while, we'd climb the spikes on telephone poles for fun. On rainy days we retreated to our spacious porches to play board games or cards. At other times, we used cellars and sometimes attics.

Though we were well sheltered from World War II, it was never far from mind. Mr. Winter, the suspected Nazi, two doors from us, sent a chill through me every time I saw him, as anything German then made people nervous. Of course, we were always reminded of the war's presence in our lives by the anti-aircraft gun and army sentry sitting visible atop Veeder Root's factory a block away. From time to time, I would tag along when ma went shopping at Stop & Shop near Sigourney Street where she would trade in coupons from her ration book for food. No butter found its way onto our shopping list, only Oleo. Some stores even sold horse meat. And for the Thanksgiving of 1944, celebrated at my aunt Mary's and uncle Jim

Sullivan's apartment, we were served roast duck, turkey being in short supply for civilians that year. I don't remember ever having duck again.

When daddy took me to a wartime submarine movie at the neighborhood Lenox Theater, he inducted me into the phony war of Hollywood movies. This was soon overshadowed by a nighttime excursion into our cellar by flashlight during a blackout.

As child warriors, we played war games incessantly, fighting against the japs and krauts, throughout the neighborhood and into the woods and hills of Keney Park. One of our favorite locations for a foxhole was the "drain," a three feet deep drainage ditch running across the back of the Johnson family's yard. Naturally, when I received a wooden, 50 mm machine gun on a tripod one Christmas during the war years, I set it up there, a commanding position on the front lines. Within a couple of days, this weapon, which produced a rat-tat-tat sound using a hand crank, broke down, much to my dismay never to be fired again. At still other times, we hurled homemade grenades--brown paper bags filled with dried up dirt over the back fences at Magnolia Street kids, our imagined enemies.

But the war really hit home the first week of July, 1944 when the Cohen-Yush family across the street lost a husband and son-in-law, David Yush, an All District quarterback at Weaver High before the war, fighting with the Marines on Saipan. Incredibly, his body would not be brought home for burial for another five years.

And in January of 1945, RM3c Tom Grady, Jr. of 6 Irving Street along with two other Connecticut men survived the sinking of their converted minesweeper in Lingayen Gulf in the Philippines and returned home safely to tell about it.

Nevertheless, much of the world suffered through the scourge of war, yet like Grady the children of my generation in Hartford remained safe and sound. Meanwhile, fifty four million souls worldwide perished.

Early in a spring morning of 1945, we were all awakened by a loud rapping on my parent's bedroom window which overlooked the driveway. Puzzled, I got up and joined them and was amazed to see and hear my Aunt Peggy Sullivan, who lived next door and had a telephone, telling my father "They want you to come in to work. The

President has died and the Times is getting out a special edition." Daddy quickly threw on some clothes and rushed off to his job.

A little later that same year, daddy walked both of us—my sister on his shoulders—downtown to celebrate VJ Day with thousands of others. I walked alongside through the delirious crowds tooting a leftover New Year's Eve horn, on the way home delighting in the chance to look in the windows of the various stores that lined Albany Avenue.

Even after the war ended it was still more of the same. After tiring of the Hardy Boys Series, so many of the first books I checked out of the library had to do with WWII. Titles like *Guadalcanal Diary,* and *The Battle for Wake Island* were popular. Boys wore sailor hats, p-coats, army hats and military divisional patches. To this day, I have saved a couple of pieces of Nazi currency given to me by my cousin Carl Polce, upon his return from the fighting in Europe. To add to this culture of war, Hollywood studios turned out movies dealing with World War II for many years in its aftermath.

Kids were hardly ever at a loss for something to do. In addition to many imaginary battles fought with the Krauts or Japs, we shot it out with the outlaws and Indians. Mimicking our movie heroes we dueled with swords fashioned from fallen tree branches. Short on money, but never ingenuity, we also made our own bow and arrows and slingshots and occasionally carved our own pistols and rifles, utilizing scrap wood.

Even used up spools of thread could be converted to play things. An empty spool with a piece of a large rubber band tied down over the opening at one end and a wooden match inserted resulted in a small rocket launcher. Owen Johnson Junior and I could sit on his front stairs and shoot these flaming missiles thirty feet or so into the air, for hours on summer nights.

Some people from my generation say they never locked their doors growing up. God bless the family that could manage that. On the contrary, my family always locked up for whatever reason and since we only had one key I remember times when I got locked out and had to climb through my first floor bedroom window to get in or sneak in through the cellar door.

Who knows now why we locked our doors because it seemed that crime was nonexistent. The only time I saw police in the 1940's was when they arrived to chase us from playing ball in the street or in later years from loitering as teens. The same can pretty much be said of the fire department. It would be years into the future, in the early 1960's, before they showed up to put out a television set "fire" (more smoke than flames) at my grandmother's house, a rare event.

I was a klutzy kid, experiencing my share of falls as a young boy. I seemed to be top heavy. Immediately after our arrival on Irving Street, I fell down the cellar stairs onto my head, as I set out to explore my new surroundings. Then there was the time I ran into the pointed corner of a dresser, hitting my forehead, just above my right eye. Worst of all was the fall I took off the back of my uncle's parked G. Fox truck and onto the sidewalk out front of our house, blood gushing everywhere. Dad rushed me to a nearby doctor's office-- my head wrapped in a towel on my own bicycle to get stitches. I still have all the scars.

Figure 11: Dad at the Hartford Times, 1939

My father, Frank Vincent Sullivan rode the bus downtown to the Hartford Times composing room roundtrip to work. When extra help was needed, he filled in as a bar tender weekends at the Garden restaurant & Grill on the corner of Garden Street and Albany, around the corner. Daddy cut through the Atlantic gas station at the corner on his way home, totting the latest copy of the N.Y. Daily News. If he noticed me in the distance, he would pop his fingers to his lips and release a loud whistle letting me know he was coming. I would immediately come running. In my mind, I can still hear and see him looking for me.

Then, there was the more bizarre. Once in a while, a stranger passing through would stop and urinate in public and then continue nonchalantly on his way. Naturally, this was shocking for a kid to see. And, there was also at least one report in the local press of child molestation at the Lenox Theater, our neighborhood movie house.

More frequently, we learned to be on guard against roaming gangs of kids from the tougher area around Clay Hill who rampaged the neighborhood looking for trouble, forcing us to the safety of our backyards.

And, in the early 1950's, a family from Maine with a daughter moved into a couple of rooms on the third floor of my friend's house. She was around my age, which at the time was thirteen. I enjoyed her company and gave her rides on my bike and she seemed to be a typical thirteen year old. So it came as a total shock when I found out she was dating a grown man and had been seen making out in his car at night under the street light in front of her lodgings. Shortly after this revelation, the family moved away.

I was very naive.

In the winter, we fought snowball battles, constructed snow forts and played King of the Royal Mountain out front of and in back of Junior Johnson's house. We sledded and skated both out in our street and at the Keney Park Pond and the Lookout, a hill we all knew well.

One time, I was outside playing when there was a lot of snow on the ground. I watched as my dad headed out of the house, wearing his fedora and scarf. The devil got a hold of me and I launched at snowball which knocked his hat off. Very calmly, dad walked over, picked me up and turned me upside down and dropped me into a snow drift.

Snow removal was a family affair involving my aunts and uncles, grandparents, ma, daddy and increasingly me. It was expected of you if you lived in one of my Nonni's houses. This involvement especially applied to shoveling our long driveway and wide backyard. Before snow blowers and plows, everything was done by hand and our homes were heated by coal. We shoveled for hours, depending on the storm and sometimes more than once. There was no getting around this. It wasn't until the late 1940's that my grandmother convinced my cousin Carl, who drove a jeep hitched to a plow for his family's garage business, to come and plow us out whenever it stormed, ending the drudgery of taking care of the driveway and yard. It also provided mountains of snow to the side of the yard, perfect for sliding and protection for launching snow ball battles with Junior Johnson, two yards away. I also enjoyed making a game out of chopping ice along the curbside, allowing water to flow freely as if creating an imaginary river.

Our coal was delivered down a chute through our cellar window into a bin where it sat until we shoveled it into the furnace. My grandmother, always on the lookout for a savings, had us sprinkle ashes from the furnace on our sidewalk when there was ice, a strategy she had picked up in her early days on the eastside. In good weather, we used coal chunks as a chalk substitute to draw on the sidewalk.

In summertime at nightfall, we were sometimes allowed out onto the front porch in our pajamas to bask in the afterglow of the day, until it got dark. After rain, we waded barefoot in our back yard. But probably our favorite activity was chasing fireflies with a jar.

Sundays, we divided up our church going three ways. We attended Sunday mass at St. Patrick Church downtown, the childhood church of my father, while at other times attending St. Anthony's Church on the eastside with my Nonni, where Father Riccio said mass in Italian. It was an unpleasant experience for me, since I did not understand Italian. More often than not, there were also times when we went to St. Joseph Cathedral on Farmington Avenue for the mandatory Children's mass. While my father still lived, we took our 1936 Dodge to these houses of worship but after his passing we simply walked with my aunts and cousin Jerome.

From time to time, the rag man, riding in a horse drawn wagon, strayed down Irving Street, calling out "rags for cash," and other come-ons, some in a foreign tongue or heavily accented English. Jerry, the mailman, brought us our mail for many years. The milkman laid milk in glass bottles with the cream at the top on our back porch. And vendors from faraway places such as Glastonbury offered vegetables and eggs from station wagons and small trucks.

We were out of the house from early morning until suppertime. There was no television, video games, cell phones or computers to distract us. Consequently, we were of necessity a creative generation. In the earliest going, I remember organizing parades using our wagons, banging on pots and pans from the house, blowing leftover New Year's horns and tooting on kazoos, up and down Irving and around the block to Magnolia Street.

On another occasion, half the neighborhood kids trekked on foot all the way downtown, through Bushnell Park, to Mulberry Street to visit the Hobby Shop. Inside, we found stamps and postcards for our growing collections and old issues of National Geographic which boys liked for the photos of topless native women. After finishing, we adjourned to the Wadsworth Atheneum to be totally amazed by the Egyptian bath tub from antiquity and the sight of real armor in the great hall. Of course, there was the added attraction of the fountain with the statue of a naked woman at center court. Finally, no trip downtown was complete without paying a visit to the Ancient Burial Ground across the street to search for Thomas Hooker's grave. Much to our delight, we found his final resting place, making us a very proud gang.

We went to bed at 7 p.m. listening to Kate Smith, The Lone Ranger, Jack Benny, Life With Luigi, Mama, Henry Aldrich and Duffy's Tavern as the evening progressed on the radio, which was located outside our door in the kitchen.

When I was nine, I was invited to a birthday party for a girl named Ellen, who was turning twelve and in sixth grade. I really looked forward to going, as it was my first invitation to anything outside of my family circle. She lived right up the street in a second floor rental, making it easy. However, when I got there, some of her older girl friends from St. Joseph School were also there mixed with some neighborhood girls, and the party quickly transitioned into Spin the Bottle. As the only boy in attendance, I quickly became the object of everyone's affections and my introduction to the world of kissing.

After spinning the bottle to a girl, we would leave for the hallway, shutting the door behind us. There, my first encounter was with a worldly sixth grade girl sprawled seductively across a love seat. *I thought, ugh a girl.* Wasting no time, she beckoned me with her fingers, drawing me to her passionately kissing and hugging me, her young cheeks flushed. She overpowered me, and would have continued having her way if the others hadn't started rapping on the living room door, anxious for their turn. I returned to them in a shocked state.

The worst of it came when the hostess herself got lucky. She was heavy and I recall thinking she would crush me. I panicked and ran to a door leading to the attic, closing it behind me, then holding onto the door knob for dear life. A tug of war commenced but after a while ended. Suddenly, it was quiet. I peeked out and seeing no one I bolted the party and ran all the way home. When I later told daddy what happened, he was very amused.

Just after World War II, a small scrawny kid wearing sun glasses and a hat with ear flaps appeared for the first time on the block by the name of Hertzel Rotenstein. *What kind of name was that, I thought.* I soon learned that it was of Eastern European origin and that his family had come to live in his aunt's house at number 9-11 Irving. They had recently arrived from displaced person's camps in Europe, being survivors of the Holocaust. He had been imprisoned in a concentration camp. Close in age, Hertzel and I became fast friends and still are.

The Rotensteins had very little when they first arrived. I think some Jewish relief agency must have given them the basics to get started with because that's all they had, just essentials—beds, dressers, a kitchen table and chairs, appliances but little else. Their living room in those days was pretty barren. *How strange, I thought, that they had no living room furniture.*

Starting then, we spent many hours together. *I can still hear him at my front door or rapping on our porch window. "Can Dennis come out?"* At first, we'd play indoors in his bedroom, on the floor and under the bed. Both of us loved sports so it was extremely exciting for both of us when he received an electric baseball game as a gift. We played that game for hours and learned to calculate major leaguers batting averages doing it.

Because of his travels in Europe, Hertzel was familiar with several languages and also spoke English well. Both his parents spoke English with accents.

His father moonlighted with a foreign package service of his own invention, at first running it out of a room in their flat. Clientele brought him things to be mailed to loved ones in Europe. As his business outgrew the house, he opened a storefront on Albany Avenue near Magnolia Street in later years. One side benefit of his European contacts was the accumulation of many postage stamps from overseas, leading to an impressive stamp collection. He stored them in stamp books several inches wide. Hertzel and I sometimes sneaked a peak into the books and were awed by what we saw, outshining our own meager collections many times over.

We played cowboys and Indians a lot and ranged far from home to the Saturday morning Kiddie Shows at the Lenox Theater at Albany Avenue and Sterling Street, with our six shooters in holsters at our sides. There we were treated to Roy Rogers, Gene Autry, Hopalong Cassidy, Superman movies, yo-yo and bubble gum contests.

I still have a fading vision of an almost mythical late fall day, heavily armed with toy pistols, sneaking into Mrs. Maule's backyard garden, then dried out by the change of seasons. Stealthily, we proceeded to set up a lean-to of branches and slipped inside awaiting the bad guys, or Indians, I can't remember which, as the season's first snowflakes blew. As the storm swirled, we fired our cap pistols at imaginary figures. In the end though, Mrs. Maule chased us away and we galloped home, chilled but ready to return and fight on another day.

Hertz and I had another adventure one snowy winter day, tramping all the way to Keney Park in snow over our arctics and then on to the Lookout, that wondrous hill, all to fight another imagined battle on the slopes.

We both loved football. In the fall, we used an under sized football that was mine for hours on end, guns practicing throwing, catching and kicking out in the street. For kicking, the wires that crossed horizontally from the telephone poles became our uprights. Hertzel was speedy and was a great pass receiver and I loved throwing to him. Of course, we both were undersized for the sport but who cared. Football became an autumn ritual for us. So did baseball and basketball in warmer weather.

If only we would clean it up first, Herzel's parents made us the generous offer of their cellar for a clubhouse. We accepted and immediately set out to sweep and clean. We did this with much gusto and little by little the place shaped up, leaving us filthy from head to foot. It was Hertzel, Frances "Tootsie" DeLucco, the street's tomboy, and I at first, with most of the Irving Street kids joining in later. I think we called ourselves "The Kings" and elected Herzel, president, and Tootsie, vice president. Though there was a side door, Hertzel and I reveled in climbing in and out through a side window, our signature entry.

Like most cellars of those times, his had a coal bin which we converted to the club library room. But a book drive we had in the neighborhood netted little. So, after giving this some thought and with my trusty red wagon in tow, we headed for the Northwest Branch of the Hartford Public Library, almost a mile away on Albany Avenue where we begged ourselves a wagon full of library discards—nothing in it of interest to kids. It was a long walk home with really little to show for our efforts.

Our next project was to raise money for a movie screen so that we could put to use the 8mm movie projector I had received for Christmas. We collected empty soda bottles and newspapers throughout the neighborhood and over time we accumulated a large pile of papers, enough to call the rags-paper dealer. He paid us about fifteen dollars for the load which allowed us to make the purchase.

In order to raise money we also set up a lemonade stand in front of my house. We sometimes sold just what the sign said, at other times Kool Aid, along with old copies of Life and Look magazines, one having nothing to do with the other. Our best customer was almost always Dominic DeLucco, the dapper city councilman and future mayor, who would drive up in his 1930's model car from his house up the street, a carnation in his lapel. This future mayor would insist on paying half a dollar for a cup which was well above the advertised five cents. And he always paid with an actual half dollar piece and a smile.

The club's variety show went well. Parents were invited and some came. A stage was constructed from scrap wood and orange crates. In the days leading up to the show, Hertzel and I walked to Church Street where there was a movie rental store and rented a couple of cartoons to show on the big night.

The highlight of the show was Herzel's magic act in which he promised to be spectacularly sawed in half. Hertzel made his successful debut. And, the big night came and went with only a minor hitch--the projector suffering a breakdown that was quickly fixed. The Parents in attendance seemed to enjoy themselves and applauded our effort.

Unfortunately, not long afterward, someone spread vicious rumors about immoral things happening in that cellar between boys and girls. Nothing of the sort was happening but it didn't seem to matter. The club's days were now numbered.

Far worse in my mind was the attack on Hertzel by a boy who had moved into the area from out of state. We both knew the kid for a while and had been to his house. Yet he never before showed signs of what was to come. The three of us were hanging out in the cellar when they began fighting, not too unusual for growing boys, but this kid came at him with a viciousness I had never encountered before. He tackled Hertz, then grabbed his head with both hands and began pounding it against the concrete floor, over and over, snarling "You dirty Jew Bastard, Kike." Horrified, I ran up the stairs to the first floor kitchen door, pounding and shouting, "Mrs.Rotenstein, Mrs. Rotenstein, Hertzel's getting killed."

When Hertzel's mother pulled them apart her voice cracked with emotion pleading, "We fled Europe to escape this. Why are you doing this?" Speechless, the boy was subsequently expelled, never to return.

Hertzel's dad bought him a basketball hoop and placed it and a backboard atop their garage. It was the first court on Irving Street, though there was another on Magnolia at the Desmairis' house, directly behind my house. We shot hoops for hours. At other times, we set up a boxing ring in his backyard, using clothes line, orange crates and kid's gloves. We'd strip down to the waist and spend the afternoon duking it out.

Holidays were celebrated to the fullest. Junior Johnson's family had relatives who occasionally showed up to celebrate the Fourth of July by blowing off dynamite caps inside trash cans and covers in his driveway. Not to be outdone, my uncles and father put on quite a fireworks annual show in our backyard setting off sky rockets, cherry bombs, and one inch firecrackers.

But it was Louie Pietro, a teen, whose family had bought the house next door in the late 1940's, who topped everyone. Originally from Clay Hill, he was still in touch with many of his friends from the old neighborhood. On the Fourth of July Eve, a carload of these kids in a 1930's black gangster style car screeched to a halt out front and began lobbing cherry bombs into the street. Not one to back down, Louie appeared on the second floor porch and unloaded his own small arsenal of Heavy duty fireworks onto his father's prized lawn, leaving a large swathe of smoking earth. For their finale, Louie's buddies pulled their getaway tossing fire crackers out car windows on both sides and departed leaving Irving Street resembling a war zone.

Being an Italian from the old country, Patsy Pietro, Louie's father, was not happy when he found out. Lawn and garden are Italian-American treasures. To see one destroyed, well…. Very soon after the incident Louie left for U.S. Army basic training.

Around the holidays, Nonni labored away in her special room in the cellar making her own homemade pasta, rolling the dough, cutting it with a big knife and hanging the pasta strips up amidst a cloud of flour. And at just about any meal, she would break out her own wine, from grapes grown at her Webster Street property—a strong concoction that demanded tempering with ginger ale when served to children.

For Easter one year my aunt Ella brought us a little, white bunny rabbit. Of course, my sister and I were thrilled and kept it in a box out on the back porch. All went well until our bunny put on weight and started to outgrow his home.

At this point, ma took control and offered our bunny to Patsy Pietro, our next-door neighbor, to add to the growing collection of pigeons and rabbits that he kept in homemade cages in his back yard.

The transfer was made in secret while we were in school one day. In the days to follow, ma concocted a new item on our supper menu, announcing the addition of lamb stew. I remember having suspicions but gave in to them and devoured what was put before me, as required. My poor unsuspecting little sister Eileen; she never thought twice about it and also ate her fill. After eating, ma casually announced to us that our supper that night had been our precious pet bunny. Hearing this, we both almost got physically sick.

We didn't have much luck with pets. Someone gave us a kitten, which we kept out in the hallway of our back porch. How we loved that kitty. Not long afterward cousin Bobby Ostiguy came over to spend the weekend. Before anyone could tell him about our kitten, Bobby stepped down into the hall and onto its head. I still recall the poor creature letting out occasional moans on my lap as Uncle Armand drove us to the Humane Society to put our pet to sleep. I was angry with my cousin afterward but it didn't last. Down deep, I knew he was completely innocent of anything.

On still another occasion, my sister received a parakeet and named him Chico. We kept him in the kitchen. Chico was a real character. Sometimes he would get loose and fly all over the house, then swoop down and end up in a dish of salad. One at least one occasion, Chico bird outdid even himself and landed in a hot pot of tomato sauce on the kitchen stove and had to be revived.

Once he even flew out the back door when my sister left the house and then followed her back inside. No one said parakeets were very smart.

For some holidays, my grandmother went out and bought a live turkey and then stored it in her cellar. When its time was up, my cousins and I rushed to watch her chase the poor creature around with an ax, eventually lopping off its head. We also watched her pluck the feathers off recently killed chickens, while sitting in the back yard, prior to dumping them in a pot of boiling water.

My father's death in the spring of 1949 threw us into an economic tailspin, taking us out of the ranks of the middle class. We were immediately reduced to a fifty-five dollar social security check each month. Incredible as it might seem, our rent was fifty dollars a month and our landlady, my tight fisted grandmother, though she had lots of rent money coming in from rental properties, refused to give us a break.

What savings we had exhausted themselves paying for daddy's funeral, plunging ma into a crisis over how we would survive. One problem was she could not hold a job anymore. Her vision had been greatly damaged in her teen years working long hours in poorly lit area sweat shops and by her mother's refusal to provide eye glasses when they could have helped, leaving her embittered and semi handicapped. By the time of my father's death, she was outfitted with very thick eye glasses.

To make matters worse, the pressure of the new normal for us made my mother a nervous wreck. It also made her hard to be around. I suppose she had to relieve the tension somehow and chose to take it out on my sister and I. She became very critical and verbally abusive. Stunad, Italian for stupid, was one of her well chosen words for me, always quick to put me down. *This was her language of love, I wondered. Can there be anything good in me?*

To help the cause, I got a Hartford Times newspaper route, or should I say ma lobbied on my behalf when she heard our newsboy of several years, Bobby Maule, was finally giving up his route at age nineteen. He had one hundred twenty customers on Irving, Magnolia and Burton Streets. However, the route was now to be divided in half and I would only get my own neighborhood with sixty customers. Anyway, I soon fell into the discipline of having cigar chomping Brick Kane and student assistant Billy Smith, an older schoolmate from St. Joe's, pull up in his big black Cadillac at my curbside and drop off a daily bundle of Hartford Times wrapped in wire for me to deliver. It brought in about twelve dollars a week—one hundred percent of which went to the family coffers—still not enough for us to get by on but a beginning.

Ma attempted a business venture of her own but it was a cockamamie scheme. She thought she could sell hot meals out of the front room window to lunch hour workers from Veeder Root Factory, two blocks away. It might have worked had we lived closer to the plant but no one would use up their lunch hour walking that distance so no one came. For a few days she tried, before admitting failure. But, as the philosophers say, necessity is the mother of all invention and she was just getting started.

Some other families on Irving Street rented out rooms, so ma decided to give it a try. We had an extra room--the front room--which led into our living room but without a wall to seal it off lacked privacy. Ma hired a carpenter to construct a wall and install a door in from the front hall. Then, using a credit line, she purchased two twin beds, and two dressers—very chic, blonde fifties furniture, better than anything we owned. She also wallpapered the room. It became a very attractive space with three windows overlooking the front porch.

One last problem needed to be solved: the only bathroom we had was near our bedrooms, only accessible through a narrow hallway from the kitchen. The bath was very small. Ma decided to postpone any solution for the time being. Instead, she purchased a classified "Room for Rent" ad in the Hartford Times and almost immediately snared her first tenants, a middle aged couple name Gaffney and their daughter in her early twenties. With them, came a new problem --that of three people and only two beds. Ma took care of that by moving me out of my bedroom and onto a cot at the end of her bed where she slept with my sister Eileen. The Gaffney's daughter got my bedroom. I was in sixth grade at the time and growing progressively angry.

But, she was getting an extra fifteen dollars a week of income, plus my paper route earnings, making us almost solvent. In years to come, she would add childcare to her growing repertoire of new found abilities. In addition to becoming a landlady, she took on lots of tasks at home—wall papering, painting, creating dresses for my sister to wear, on her sewing machine. I can still see her sitting next to a side window squinting desperately with her fading vision trying to thread her needle so she could patch our clothes.

Luckily for me, I wasn't the only one who didn't take to the new living arrangement and after several months the Gaffneys moved out. Over the next couple of years, ma rented to a single mom with child, a single woman and finally a newly married couple, the husband a descendant of General George McClellan, Army of the Potomac. They were from out of state and came to Hartford to work in the insurance business. The wife was a blonde and very attractive.

Getting into our bathroom continued to be a problem, especially in the mornings. It irked me to see the husband in his bath robe and shower clogs, slogging through our house on his way to use the bathroom, like some college guy living in a fraternity house. His demeanor wasn't the only thing I resented about him. Seeing that I had grown increasingly out of the control for my poor mother, our roomer next decided on intervention.

Probably well meaning, he confronted me in the kitchen. I told him to back off and fled into our cellar. Unbelievably, he chased me and tried to take up where he left off. I screamed at him "You are not my father," as tears welled in my eyes. Seeing he could not prevail, he gave up and never bothered me again. Still, maybe it would have been good for me if he had.

Eventually, ma hired Sam Testa, my uncle, to convert the front bedroom closet to a bathroom with a stand up shower. It turned out quite nice and I used it myself at times when the room was vacant.

We survived without a telephone at home until I was in my junior high school years, at first a two party line. My aunt Margaret Sullivan had one next door and my father had given out our phone number at work for emergencies.

Our first phone was a two party landline situated in the small hallway between the bedroom and bathroom hallway. When my mother wasn't around, it was fun eavesdropping on people we didn't know from surrounding neighborhoods, as long as no one got caught which never happened.

The only time we received an emergency call was the time when FDR died in springtime, 1945, and my aunt came over and rapped noisily on my parent's bedroom window waking me up.

Toward the end of grammar school, my friend Herzel and I concocted a lame brained scheme to trick my friend Mike Angellilo into believing a major league team had an interest in him, after he'd pitched a no hitter for our team in the Jay Cee Courant League. Out of jealousy or juvenile perversity, probably both, we created a letter on Hertzel's newly acquired portable typewriter while sitting on his front porch. Supposedly written by a Cleveland Indians scout, the letter said he had noticed Mike's performance and a tryout might be forthcoming. Mike was ecstatic when he got our letter so much so that he showed it to Fr. John Shugrue, our principal. Upon reading it, and noticing the odd use of red and black ribbons, plus spelling and grammatical errors, Father asked, "Mike, do you really believe this?"

Perhaps penance for my participation in this caper came when I failed to make the St. Joe's baseball team. Like many boys who loved the game, my Illusions exceeded my abilities--I really wasn't very talented and I choked at tryouts. The same failure happened with Little League tryouts, too. When the time for the first Hartford Little League Parade rolled around, I found myself on the outside looking in, as some schoolmates strutted by in brand spanking new uniforms in downtown Hartford. I was heartbroken.

My mother continued her hypercritical attitude towards me. We probably both needed help but didn't get any.

Nearing the end of grammar school at St. Joe's, I found myself coping by growing defiant, fighting back, leading to many shouting matches and much unpleasantry between us. Faced with unhappiness and tension at home, I increasingly took to the streets as high school loomed.

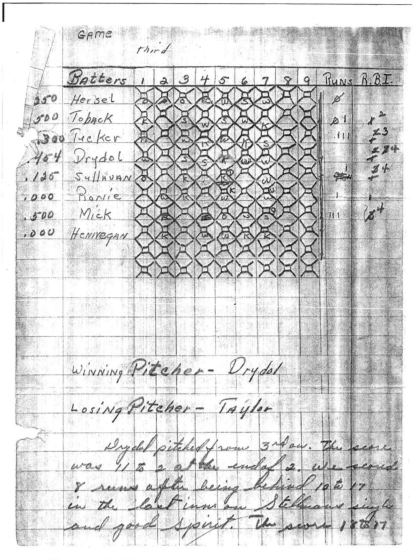

Figure 12: Ed Dryol's Scorebook, early 1950's

Baseball

My dad was a huge New York Yankee's fan. As a boy he played baseball growing up on the eastside and learned to love the game. Quite naturally he wanted to impart that love to me, his only son, as I grew up. It started with our playing catch in the backyard, then extended into drives to Keney Park to watch amateur and semi-pro games, none of which I was happy about; I wanted to be back on Irving Street playing non-baseball type games. Instead, I actually got angry with him and begged to be returned to my friends. But daddy never gave up. He even bought me a kid's size Yankee jacket, which at least I liked and wore to school. Even so, his efforts mostly failed. When I did finally embrace the game, it was after much screaming and kicking.

Almost everyone in my extended family of aunts, uncles, and cousins also rooted for the Yankees, with one notable exception, my first cousin Paul who was a supporter of the Boston Red Sox. How he got that way remains a mystery but we still loved him.

The year my father died I was ten years old. That spring, during bouts with measles and mumps and mourning, nothing changed in my attitude regarding baseball. I was still disinterested. However, that summer my Uncle Sam Testa, a stalwart Yankee supporter, now living with his own growing family upstairs in a second floor rental, took me to see my first major league game in New York.

I was all excited about the trip and remember thinking I'd see a lot of the famous New York skyline close up. Disappointingly, the ride down was uneventful and we neared Yankee Stadium without sight of any skyscrapers. I was starting to feel chagrined.

Then Sam said, "We're going to see banana nose." *I could tell this tickled his fancy. I thought, who could banana nose be and who would want a name like that?* Before I could pose the question, Sam smiled and said, "Banana nose is Joe DiMaggio." Only my uncle, creator of names for people and things-- most especially his cars-- would come up with Jolting Joe DiMaggio nomenclature, the first and last time I've ever heard DiMaggio referred to in that way.

Actually I'm now aware that another major league player, Zeke Bonura of the Chicago White Sox had once been called banana nose, a fact that could not have escaped my uncle's attention, being originally from the Chicago area himself... but not Joe D. Thanks, Sam.

That summer I fell madly in love with the national pastime, both as a player and as a fan. Following the family tradition, the Yankees became my team of choice and from then on many of my free hours were consumed with a bat, ball and glove. Daddy would have loved it.

At first it was only backyard stickball at Eddie Drydol's on Sargeant Street with Mike Angelillo and Eddie Kotulski. If we didn't have a ball we'd roll paper into a ball and wrap it with adhesive tape. We went at it for hours without interruption until the ball ended up on the garage roof, prematurely ending our outing or we simply called it a day.

Then, back in my own neighborhood, Tootsie, Hertzel and I took the game into the street and backyards of Irving Street, notably the Johnson and Yush yards, as mini-diamonds, officially thirty three feet wide. We were joined by any kid of any age that could be recruited—Eddie Yush, Jr. Johnson, the Kahn's, Mary and Joan Williams, Bobby and Jerry Stroh, Danny Larensen, Judy Simons, my sister Eileen and occasionally Bobby Maule. We chose up sides using a bat, hand over hand, with Tootsie DeLucco, who was as a skilled player as any boy, being in biggest demand.

For equipment we had a motley collection of well-worn, hand me down bats and gloves and used any ball available—rubber, tennis, softball and baseball. Usually for street ball, we didn't use a baseball because of the risk of breaking windows in the close quarters.

Lots of times we hiked to Keney Park to play ball during summer and school vacations. For close by alternatives we played at Vine Street schoolyard, which, though small, also had a rough diamond at the far end, as did Weaver High School on the corner with Blue Hills and Westborne Parkway.

In earliest times, our street challenged kids from Magnolia, the next street over to games, after that teaming up with school chums and graduating to real sand lot games against kids from other neighborhoods. This frequently involved intra-city travel. Pope Park comes to mind as the scene of one of our earliest contests versus a team from Frog Hollow, organized by a schoolmate from St. Joe's. Kids arranged their own games then. I still remember pedaling my bike there with Eddie Drydol on the cross bar and carrying a bat and gloves, a good couple of miles from home. We thought nothing of the distance. Elizabeth and eventually Colt's Park became destinations, too.

Later on in grammar school, I played with boys from school on a dirt lot behind the old Stop and Shop near Sigourney and Albany and just about anywhere there was enough space. Sigourney Square (aka Sigourney Park) and St. Joe's schoolyard were also options, though the last one only sporadically as it was too far away and small.

Backyard play with a tennis ball, the forerunner of whiffle ball, was played under highly constricted conditions because of the smallness of the yards. Many times we were hitting homers and had to retrieve the ball from the next street over. When no games were available, I'd practice alone in the backyard throwing a tennis ball against the back wall.

Individually, Eddie Drydol and I played together a lot, sometimes at his house, sometimes in my driveway. Courtesy of the Morris boys, I owned a cast off catcher's mitt and we'd take turns pitching to each other. Other times we trekked to Keney Park, setting up in front of the tennis courts for a backstop, one-on- one. On separate occasions, we'd go deeper into the park on our bikes and practice on the outfield grass near Diamond One.

Once the snow melted, even if the ground was still wet, we'd get out there. Leading up to this as winter subsided, I would prep my glove for the coming season, oiling the pocket with olive oil, then pounding it in. Afterward, I'd position a baseball in it and move it onto my dresser top, waiting for any sign of spring.

One of us would hit, while the other pitched. We had our own well defined ways of telling what were hits or runs. For instance, any time you dropped or bobbled a playable ball, it was a hit. Hits and runs, just like in the real game. We also named our teams: Yankees or Red Sox, Braves, and so on. It was our own form of fantasy baseball. We could select anyone we wanted for our teams: Joe DiMaggio, Stan Musial, Ted Williams, Phil Rizzutto, Yogi Berra, Willie Mays, as long as we didn't pick a player the other kid already had. But what a rush selecting players was--having the power to pick all stars, future hall of famers, on your team!

By today's standards, our equipment was primitive. Gloves were flat with only webbing barely big enough to catch a ball. For bats we had hand me down beat up wooden ones. My most memorable one I inherited from my Uncle Joe Russo after he died of cancer—a 36 inch Louisville Slugger with a crack on the handle. Way too heavy but if playing slow pitch and making a connection— lots of pop and excitement, the crack notwithstanding.

In junior high school, we formed a team and joined the Jay Cee Courant League that played its games in Colt's Park. Mike, Eddie and I were members of that squad. I think we won our first game 14-0, cause for lots of boyish celebration. But our jubilation quickly turned sour with one loss after another, culminating in an 18-0 debacle against the Caval Tool Bobcats, a towering team of kids from New Britain who could power the ball deep into the outfield and who featured a pitcher named Steve Dalkowski, reputedly one of the fastest of any all time.

Beginning in the 1953 season, Caval Tool went on to win forty three consecutive games, impressive in any era. Steve later had a pro career and at one point clocked over 100 mph. Imagine how it felt to only be able to hear the ball as it popped in the catcher's mitt and not be able to see it. That's what it was like facing Dalkowski. It turned out he was wild, though and sent our buddy Eddie to the emergency room of the hospital after hitting him in the head. In the end, that first season was a disaster during which we never won another game. Charlie Brown would have fit right in.

For the next several seasons we entered a team in the Courant League with Ed, Mike and I being the core members. One year we were the State Glass Nine, another the Lipman Ramblers, all losers. The roster of kids playing with us would change from year to year depending on who was available. In all that time and adversity though, we never gave up hope. I loved the game and never missed practice with the guys, even though I had little to show for it in actual games. We drew boys from HPHS, Bulkeley, Weaver and Bloomfield. And I got to meet and be teammates with kids I would never have otherwise.

Nevertheless, I never amounted to much as a player and my expectations always exceeded my abilities. I wasn't a skilled hitter or fielder and it didn't help that, out of vanity I'm sure, I usually refused to wear my eye glasses. Being very near sighted and playing without spectacles had to hurt my game.

On the field, my greatest strength was getting on base. I was patient at the plate and held off swinging at bad pitches. So I walked a lot. This gave me the opportunity for steals. (If you know anything about youth baseball you know young pitchers are bothered by control problems and catchers can't throw anyone out.) I wasn't that fast on the base paths but I would dangle myself off first base and try to bother the pitcher by yelling some time honored bait like "Hey, pitcher, pitcher." When things looked good or the catcher choked, "I'd go." I was never thrown out, though sometimes sliding in.

In the summer of 1955, we finally got our due. Mike and I combined to recruit probably the best roster of players in our history including Johnny Egan, Eddie Lowndes and Joel Millstein. At the time I was working after school in the stock room at Seaboard Record Distributors behind the Stop & Shop at Albany Avenue and Sigourney Street. I told my two supervisors we were looking for coaches and both men agreed to check out our first practice. One was a short, chain smoking guy from Brooklyn, N.Y., who we called Little Joey, to distinguish him from the other man, also named Joe, chain smoker down to butts and African American. Both showed up but only Little Joey liked what he saw and took over the reins.

Opening day for league play was fast approaching and we still didn't have a name for our team. I remember talking about it to Eddie and others as we walked from Diamond one to Diamond two at Keney Park for out next practice. I suddenly had a brainstorm. "How about the Crewcuts? We could all get crewcuts and use that name for our team." ("Sh-Boom," by the Crewcuts was my favorite tune at the time). We put in the paper work with the League and that's who we became and most of us sported crewcuts for the season.

Eddie Lowndes liked to pitch our batting practice and used to get me very upset throwing a steady diet of curve balls, which he knew I couldn't hit. *C'mon Ed, give something I can hit, I pleaded. It's batting practice, for crying out loud.* He never did. I think he did it to irritate me and he succeeded.

Since most of us didn't yet have driver's licenses, our coach, Little Joey provided chauffer service before and after games, ranging from Blue Hills Avenue to Irving Street, picking us up and bringing us right to our doors. Each week during the season he crammed several sweaty, smelly teenage boys into his undersized car and transported us to Colt's Park on the other side of town. What a guy!

That year, 1955, would be the only year we'd enjoy a winning season. In the early going, we suffered a ten inning loss 3-2, at the hands of Our Lady of Sorrows. Regrouping afterward and led by the stellar pitching of Egan, Lowndes and Angelillo, we advanced to win our division sporting a 4-1 record and made it into the League Semi Finals before being bounced by the Heublein A-1 Aces. I sat on the bench most of that game until being put in late as a pinch hitter only to ground out. It was the best team I ever played on.

In one of our games against the Capitol City Lumberjacks, a winning effort, Johnny Egan hit an inside the ballpark homerun. He was so quick on the bases.

Thirty years later, I ran into Little Joey who was working at a local business and all he wanted to talk about was that summer when he coached our pitcher John Francis Egan, future basketball All-American and NBA player, his big moment as a coach.

My baseball playing days ended that summer but baseball wasn't totally through with me, opening doors for me after high school. When I was stationed in the Pacific Northwest in the United States Air Force, I volunteered to write a sport's column for the base newspaper, even though I had barely survived English classes at Weaver High and had no experience whatsoever writing for publication.

One of my first assignments was covering the base baseball team. As part of that responsibility, I traveled with the team to different ball fields inside Washington State and British Columbia, usually by USAF bus but sometimes in a C-47 Gooney Bird airplane. Even though lacking in writing experience I discovered I knew enough about the sport that I could do a halfway decent job of it. Others noticed and when the editor of the base newspaper was shipped to Iceland, I was promoted to that position, transferring me out of a boring job as a clerk in the base housing office toward the end of my second year of service. I was thrilled at this opportunity.

Other doors opened up for me, too. After being discharged from the Air Force, the editorial experience helped me get accepted into the University of Hartford full-time in the fall of 1961, designated as a student on probation but with potential.

Three and a half years later, I graduated with a bachelor's degree in English. Two summers later, my background harking back to my sport's writing days helped me land a summer job as public information officer for the Community Renewal Team (CRT) in Hartford. And several years later, I landed that same position, full time, for South Central Community College in New Haven.

After all was said and done, baseball had paid off in ways my father could never have imagined all those years before when he tried his best to interest me in the game.

SANDLOT HALL OF FAME

Players: Bobby Jordan, Ricky Marchese, Mike Angellilo, Eddie Drydol, Eddie Kotulski, Bobby T, Billy Dausch, Johnny Egan, Eddie Lowndes, Joel Milstein, Gerry Falvey, Tony Rinaldi, Bobby Murray, Bobby Tomalonis, George Bell, Cecil Gaston, Tommy Radigan, Bobby Higgins, Bobby Rice, Neal Moylan, Tom Shea, Herb Toback, Mike Heneghan, Bobby Monroe, George Delaney, Billy Quinten, Carl Jarvis, Clem Langlois, Hertzel Rotenstein, Dave Murray, Dave Johnson, Mick Tucker..

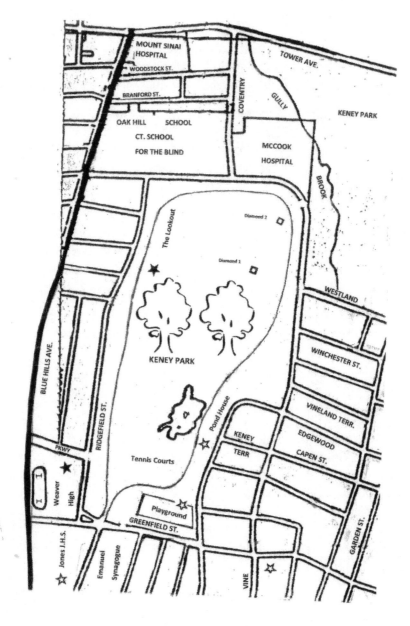

BLUE HILLS - KENEY PARK AREA

1955

Figure 13: 1950s Map

The Lenox Theater

Until World War I, Albany Avenue remained largely a residential area, so it was no surprise that it wasn't until June 7, 1925—as part of accelerated commercial development and population growth--- that movies came to the North End with the opening of the Lenox Theater on the corner of Albany and Sterling with an announced capacity of approximately 1,000. Within months of the Lenox's construction the Colonial was soon rising on Farmington Avenue and, though unrelated, the legendary State Theater was going up in the downtown center. This development came almost two decades after movies first arrived in Hartford in a theater on Main Street called "The Nickel."

Back then, when radio was young and television was a science fiction writer's dream, the Lenox Theater quickly became a fixture in North End life as a second run theater. Once movies finished their run in downtown movie houses like the palatial Loew's Poli, they were next redistributed to neighborhood theaters like the Lenox and Colonial.

Opening night in 1925, with many career movie men from around the state in attendance, featured a picture, *The Talker,* news reels, a comedy and scene pictures, plus a musical program, with the performance to begin at eight o'clock. The Lenox management booked its own orchestra for the evening in a performance of "Prince of Pilsen" conducted by F.A. Wilbur. Violin soloist, Albert Card, was also booked to play several pieces.

Every day following the Grand Opening a matinee was scheduled for 2 pm and two shows each evening beginning at 6:30 and 8 pm, the routine in those earliest years. Back then, price of tickets was ten cents which got you two feature films, a Pathe newsreel and a serial. Later on, cartoons were added to the menu.

Gradually over the years, prices rose so that in the mid thirties "Top Hat" with Fred Astaire and Ginger Rogers would cost thirty five cents. By 1960, admission reached seventy to seventy five cents, evenings M-F between 6:15-7 p.m., and children's tickets shot up from twenty five to thirty cents. Of course, prices varied according to shows: matinee or evenings, early bird specials from 6:15 – 7 p.m., and kiddie show prices. Occasionally a program was free, especially if it was a documentary about a timely subject like health care, as the Lenox prided itself in being a community educator.

The original marquee for the new theater was rectangular with large letters denoting *LENOX, very* different from the exterior of my childhood in the late 1940's and 1950's when the theater boasted a v-shaped marquee with an eighteen foot spread on both arms and a vertical "LENOX" joining them. At the time of its opening, it was believed by management to be the largest marquee of its kind in the city, perhaps a somewhat dubious distinction, as the State Theater also soon laid claim to that title and more justifiably so, having one that stretched a long way up Village Street. The interior of the new theater had a distinctive overhead dome and, in the early going at least, elevated box seats situated off of both sides of the stage.

During the silent movie era, the Lenox owned an Austin organ and hired a player to provide accompaniment for its screen offerings. Area moviegoers flocked to "the Lenox habit," as it was being advertised, to be entertained by the great stars of the 1920's: Wallace Beery, Clara Bow, Mary Pickford, Doug Fairbanks, Rudolph Valentino, Lon Chaney, Gloria Swanson, Greta Garbo, Norman Shearer, Lionel Barrymore, Paul Muni and Adolphe Menjou, unforgettable celluloid characters many local movie goers would remember fondly the rest of their lives.

Not unlike the multi dimensional nature of today's minor league baseball parks and at times seemingly in the spirit of P.T. Barnum, right from the onset the Lenox opened its doors to the local community, offering more than movies---for area moviegoers and, in particular, but not exclusively for Upper Albany and Blue Hill's residents.

In the 1920's, the theater hosted a whirlwind of talks, programs and parties. In January, 1926, a Dr. Millard Knowlton gave a lecture titled, "The Beginning of Life," starting up what was hoped would be free films and talks on the last Sunday of each month for the educational advancement of the population. Meanwhile, the local Motherhood Club was invited in for a showing, as guests of the house in that same time frame, as the Lenox was looking to attract more families.

For St. Patrick's Day fare in 1926, Arnold and Dotty, a novelty act of live song and dance and "Irish Luck," and an Irish sketch was featured on the house stage. That same spring the Lenox announced an "International Week for Charity" benefiting, French, German, Jewish and Irish groups.

In the fall, a popular movie, "Padlocked" arrived at the Lenox after a successful run at the Lowe's Poli Palace downtown weeks before. For its first two nights, as a public relation's gimmick, Doris Beaupre, "Miss Hartford, 1926," was padlocked in the foyer and only paying customers could save her. To this end, patrons then received keys to see who could free Miss Beaupre.

The next year, now a free woman, the same Miss Beaupre was rehired for a return engagement, this time to stand in the theater's lobby holding a sign advertising the then current movie.

That same year the Lenox opened its doors to hundreds of Northwest School District Boy Scouts for a lecture and Christmas party, welcomed a local Republican rally, hosted an afternoon of Hebrew opera and folk music with Miro Glass which was billed in the press as "The Big Jewish Meeting" with proceeds to help rebuild Palestine. The theater further hosted two Passover plays with a cast of many and music to benefit the Hebrew Women's Home for Children.

Another community outreach event allowed fundraising for Camp Courant and Almeda Lodge also in 1927, providing space for a table-booth out front staffed by two Cabot Street girls and a Homestead Avenue boy, the Lenox generously matching whatever funds they raised.

Other events in the twenties featured Christmas parties, the live stage debut of Ben Rosenberg and Maude Weaver, a song and dance act twice a night for a two day stand, also a Juvenile Fiddle Contest the competition taking three nights with cups given as prizes, a Mary Pickford look-alike contest with cash prizes, and on an afternoon in 1927 a free documentary film, *House of Mercy.* Not to be outdone by competitors, the Lenox even sponsored its own basketball team, at one point losing to its much bigger downtown rival, Lowe's.

There was also a Paramount Week featuring a spate of Paramount films—Clara Bow in *The Redhead* on one day and a very young Gary Cooper in *The Legion of the Condemned,* as one of several other offerings. Then there were Revival Weeks reshowing classic movies---for instance, *The Three Musketeers* with Douglas Fairbanks, and Mary Pickford in *Little Lord Fauntleroy*---and vacation weeks focused on special showings for area kids during school breaks.

Many of the blockbuster hits of the era graced the Lenox screen: Rudolph Valentino in *The Sheik,* Charlie Chaplin in *The Kid,* the original *Ben Hur,* Gloria Swanson in *Stage Struck,* Greta Garbo in *Torrent* playing a Spanish maid, Cecil B. DeMille's original *Ten Commandments* and D.W. Griffith's *America.*

Nonetheless, a goodly number of schlock movies made their way to the Lenox screen: *Goose Women, Why Girls Go Back Home, Mother Machree, Rose of the Tenements, Bluebeards Seven Wives, We're in the Navy Now, Stranded in Paris, Casey at the Bat and Flaming Frontier* come to mind. Tom Mix and his wonder horse,Tony, passed through the Lenox in a feature, E*verlasting Whisper,* around the same time.

Of course the movie going rage of the twenties was the introduction of sound, or talkie movies. After premiering in New York in the fall of 1927 with Al Jolson's *The Jazz Singer,* talkies finally reached the Lenox in late April 1928. What followed was a succession of highly advertised sound version extravaganzas at the Lenox: Al Jolson again in *The Singing Fool (*March 22, 1929), the first offering at the Lenox using Vitaphone, a process in which the sound track was recorded on 33 1/3 rpm records and played simultaneously with the movie; *Abbie's Irish Rose* (March 31, 1929); the spectacular, *Broadway Melody,* billed as All Talking, All-Singing, All Dancing from

MGM; Movietone *Follies of 1929,* a Talkie musical (July 14, 1929); and *Cock-eyed World* from Fox Movietone, topping the billings.

During the Depression years, the Lenox played host to Passover plays with large casts of locals and "The Wedding of Tom Thumb,"which was a juvenile review boasting a cast of sixty neighborhood kids (thirty in the chorus alone) on the theater's stage for three performances in 1933. There was a Holcomb Street School PTA fundraiser for books and cod liver oil for needy Holcomb Street neighborhood pupils in 1935, and live Amateur Nights that ran on stage for twelve weeks with cash prizes in the cash strapped thirties. At Christmas time, bonneted Salvation Army workers with bells braved the elements outside the theater soliciting for the city's needy.

An older Irving Street boy once recounted to me how he was at the Lenox for the matinee performance on Sunday, December 7, 1941, when the house lights suddenly came on and a theater employee got up on the stage and informed everyone present that the country was now at war. Soon the Lenox would be doing its bit in aiding the war effort by organizing a war bond sales drive annually. Those who stepped up and bought bonds got in admission free for the day of the purchase. Scrap metal drives for the war effort were also carried out there on a regular basis, seventeen million pounds being needed nationally.

It was during the war years that I saw my first Hollywood movie at the Lenox accompanied by my father in 1943. The feature film was a sub movie, *Crash Drive,* featuring Dana Andrews and Ty Powers. It was the first of many Lenox visits.

Both my parents enjoyed seeing movies and while my dad was alive we attended movies as a family, sometimes strolling the five blocks, sometimes riding in our car; because of gas rationing for the war effort, walking was preferred. Clearly, the Lenox habit, as some called it, was our habit.

And during this decade, the Lenox also became " the habit" for teenagers Norman Lear, future film and television producer; Totie Fields, comedian; and Eileen McClory, a Holcomb Street tomboy, later turned Conover model for covers of Vogue, Mademoiselle and Harpers magazines (and Hollywood movie starlet) with fond rembrances of Jimmy Stewart movies at the Lenox in the late thirties; and finally, comedian-actor, Charles Nelson Reilly.

From this bunch, it may have been Reilly who was most captivated by the Lenox. Indeed, in his later years, it would be Reilly who frequently expressed gratitude to Lenox house manager Kate Treske for her early influence on his career in show business. As he remembered it in his one man show, "Life of Reilly," it was Mrs. Treske who anointed him as an actor inside her office at the Lenox, when Reilly was still a student at Weaver High.

My own generation best remembers this same Mrs.Treske as the no-nonsense, reigning house manager of the Lenox. On the job, she scrutinized closely every kid coming through the Lenox door, the good, and, more importantly, the troublemakers. It was her job to know who was who and she did.

Quite naturally with teen boys in particular there was always cause for concern---boys acting up, fighting, sneaking buddies in side doors. In her two piece suit and carrying a flash light Mrs. Treske was always poised for the fray and many's the wobegon boy who got her boot back onto Albany Avenue.

Mrs. Treske was one of the longest lasting house managers in a succession of heads dating back to the Lenox's earliest time. She also may have been the only woman to hold the job. Generally, men with names like Sanson, Glassman, Cummings, Campbell, D'Aprea, and even Treske's own husband, Nathaniel, were placed in charge. There was also unfortunate Gustave Schaefer, treasurer for the Lenox Management Corporation and former executive overseas for Paramount and RKO, who died at his desk at the Lenox in 1953.

Two of the scariest movies I've ever seen played the Lenox when I was still in grammar school---*The Cat People* and *The Thing from Outer Space*. Even now, I recall the fright I felt from their fearful black and white images and shadow effects. My kid sister, Eileen, came with me to see *The Thing* and was quickly so petrified that I had to wrap my arms around her, eyes shut unable to look. Though I was three years older, I had all I could do to keep my own cool.

As far as *The Cat People* goes, I think I had nightmares for weeks after seeing it. And, black and white made horror movies more horrifying.

Throughout the lifetime of the Lenox, there continued a spirit of openness, adaptability and community cooperation. Later on in the 1940's, weekly Saturday morning Kiddie Shows not only featured a serial, cartoons, and feature movies--- Roy Rogers, Gene Autry, Hopalong Cassidy were favorites, but sometimes a yo-yo or bubble gum blowing contest or a live act with a local cowboy entertainer and a horse also kept kids coming.

In November of 1947, just in time for my ninth birthday, I returned home from the Lenox happily waving a Tom Mix humming lariat souvenir, one of 4,500 giveaways at the kiddie shows of five local movie theaters. Westerns were big favorites then, especially with boys, and sometimes I remember my friend Hertzel and I packing our plastic six shooters in our holsters to wear to the kiddie show, then riding off on our fantasy horses heading home. Hi, ho, Silver!

In 1951 radio personality Joe Girard (WTHT Radio) and Brother Rabbit appeared on stage. In 1964, the Five Satins performed at the Lenox as part of a revue. Gospel music came to the Lenox in the mid 1960's and the Rehoboth Church of God held services there briefly in 1967.

There were several episodes of mismanagement of the theater. One of the most shocking was its foreclosure sale just over a year into its lifetime in July 1927 after accumulating debts of ninety thousand dollars and a first mortgage of seventy two thousand. In a last minute deal Park Investment, also owners of the Lyric, purchased the Lenox for two hundred fifty thousand dollars, saving it from being auctioned off. Over the years, the Lenox suffered through several more ownership upheavals, usually being sold off to local holding corporations. One of the final sell offs occurred in 1963 when it sold again to Allied Associates for eighty thousand dollars, a far cry from the glory days of the twenties.

Throughout its lifetime, the Lenox also endured bouts with crime, juvenile delinquency and bizarre behavior. In the first of these episodes in May, 1930 a supernumerary cop out on evening patrol called for back up after finding the Lenox side door open. Like a scene from a Keystone Cops movie, a wagon-load of cops answered the call and then stormed the theater with weapons, automatic and otherwise, drawn. The men in blue then preceded to search the inside with flashlights, cellar to rooftop. In the midst of the search and after hearing someone cough, the police searched the balcony, only to discover two local newspaper reporters in hiding up there; the pair in question had gotten to the "crime scene" ahead of the cops and may have been hoping for a scoop. The only other person they uncovered that night was the supernumerary himself, safe and sound inside the theater's office guarding the safe.

Without a doubt, the most bizarre occurrence in Lenox history struck on a cold late afternoon and evening in October of 1939 when five year old Ann Slovkin of 50 Mansfield Street disappeared after telling her sister she was going to the theater's rest room. Police were immediately called and a search of the Lenox commenced with northend resident, Detective Thomas C. Barber playing a major role. Barber and others were then dispatched to Mansfield Street where they searched the girl's home and neighborhood, including every parked car on the street, since Ann had previously been known to enjoy slipping into vehicles. The search even extended out into Keney Park without success. Local radio stations called for the public's assistance.

Coming seven years after the famous Lindbergh kidnapping case, the possible abduction of a young northend girl undoubtedly must have spooked parents all over the city.

Two hours later a cop making an arrest for drunken driving in Plainville found the Slavkin girl, unhurt, but shivering in the chilly evening air, without coat or hat, lying in the back of a truck. At first, the driver, Selwyn Simons, 31, of Cornwall Bridge claimed she was his daughter but quickly retracted that story, then saying he had invited her into his truck along with two other girls in Hartford. Apparently, Ann was the only one to accept.

Simons, who also claimed he belonged to a cult pledged to end "children's misery," identified his residence as Joy Farms and his occupation as secretary of the Emma Curtis Hopkins Fund, a foundation established by a leading 19th century spiritualist whose teachings would soon have a great influence on the founders of Alcoholics Anonymous.

Incredibly, he was only charged with "enticing a minor female," got fined one hundred dollars and given a suspended three month jail sentence, then released. Enticing in the late thirties carried sentence parameters of a five hundred dollar fine, or five years in jail, or both.

In the summer of 1946, a 35 year old Walnut Street man came on to a young woman sitting in front of him at the Lenox with her mother. The daughter said he kept trying to lean over the seat. He said he was just trying to "get acquainted" and charged with breach of the peace.

A local teen started a fight with the doorman in the fall of 1951, after being ejected for causing trouble. Some teens in the audience then took sides and the emergency doors opened and the crowd left. When the police arrived no one would share any information.

Trying to sneak in a side door opened by a friend, fighting, throwing things and acting up kept the Lenox staff busy, especially in the fifties. I did get bounced a couple of times for screwing around. But most of my time there on Friday and Sunday nights with buddies alongside the blue Carino's Gas Station illuminated clock hanging from the wall, our preferred seating, was spent in serious movie enjoyment. Pictures like *Shane, Singing in the Rain, Friendly Persuasion, Battleground and The Student Prince* entertained and delighted me.

Once, in my senior year of high school though, as I exited the Lenox with my pal Richie McGill, out of nowhere he got into a scrap with Eddie, another Weaver senior, duking it out in full teenage fury under the marquee surrounded by a curious crowd of teens. It happened so quickly, seemingly without a flash point, I was stunned. I didn't see it coming, not at all. Perhaps I was busy still replaying the evening's movie in my head. It was over as fast as it started. And both boys walked away still standing.

The State Theater never dared to book Elvis Presley, management believing him too explosive for local audiences. But the Lenox did welcome him with open arms, much to the delight of many north end fans in early January, 1958 when *Jailhouse Rock,* the MGM film starring Elvis, opened to some of the largest crowds ever at the Lenox, the ticket line extending around the corner onto Sterling Street.

Over its first thirty five years, the Lenox had gained status as a community hub and geographical landmark on Albany Avenue--- telephone: 522-2911---so much so that most of the nearby businesses would always link onto the Lenox in their newspaper advertising. For instance, my uncle Emil Polce, owner of a well-known auto repair business on Cabot Street very close by, would add a tag to his ads: "Just a step from Albany right next to the Lenox Theater." At one point, some local businesses even began co-hosting events; for example, Carino's Cities Service station, one block away, promoted a "Santa is Coming in Person" Christmas event---Gifts, Candy and Free Movie Tickets in December of 1963.

As the sixties unfolded, the Lenox continued doing its bit as a responsible community resource. Taking full advantage of this, the Vine Street School PTA ran a movie fundraiser with the Lenox, a movie series with some of the proceeds to benefit the PTA. *Dance With Me Henry, Bonzo Goes to College, Lone Ranger, War Drums* were some of the offerings. Beth Sholom PTA also ran a fundraiser there with proceeds to Camp Ramah Scholarship Fund, and Rawson School PTA co-hosted a series of weekly films with the proceeds going to educational projects.

However, the sixties were not kind to the Lenox. In the summer of 1960, the theater had to be emptied because of a telephoned anonymous bomb threat. The police and fire department were summoned and the Lenox searched but nothing was found.

Perhaps as a further sign of the times, in 1961, an unidentified man walked up to the box office and demanded cash. A quick thinking cashier, Jane Rutherford, then slammed the box office window down on the man's hand, setting off an alarm buzzer. Hearing this, Bruce Monde, the doorman, gave chase but lost the culprit more than once and finally for good.

The same year patrons were treated to a terror-filled B movie double bill: *Asylum of Horrors, House of the Living Dead with Dracula* with extras *The Ethereal Form of Marilyn Monroe Materialized* plus *The Earthly Apparition of Elvis Presley*---with the proviso: "Free two for one passes if you can sit through it" and a giveaway I.D. bracelet for all girls.

The small crime incidents continued throughout those years. As part of a revenge plot in 1964 by teens for having been thrown out of the theater the summer before, some boys broke into the Lenox using screwdrivers, knocked the dial off the office safe, and took over forty dollars from a soft drink machine. They also left behind a note warning of another possible future attack.

In the midst of declining times, *The Longest Day* and *The Great Escape*, notable WWII films, passed through as did *El Cid* with Sophia Loren and Charlton Heston and a Charlie Chaplin revival showing of *The Gold Rush* with music and dialog added, accompanied by a Harold Lloyd comedy. *King Kong V.S. Godzilla* also found its way there.

In July of 1965, the theater appealed to the public for clothing and furniture for eight families who had recently been burned out of their Albany Avenue apartments. Then, the Lenox seems to have closed for a short while before reopening under new management and renamed "The New Lenox," who now envisioned a double role of movie house and live entertainment venue. The new owners looked to attract arts festivals, gospel shows and other cultural programs. It also booked rock 'n' roll shows. All this and movies, too.

Two years later, the demise of the Lenox was brought into focus by a "For Sale, For Lease" ad in the Hartford Courant, promoting a theater as a possible dancehall, night club or billiard parlor. The advertising practically offered to give the once mighty theater away.

That summer a "Crusade for Christ" was announced for the Lenox featuring Arturo Skinner and a 500-voice choir but at the last minute the program was switched to a local church.

In the fall of that same year, 1967, following a live stage show, a crowd of teenagers gathered outside and demanded their money back. Police in numbers were called after a single cop was unable to get things under control. A girl and a boy were arrested at the scene and charged with breach of the peace. The stage show was closed down.

The following winter, in a now vacant Lenox, the Hartford Fire Department responded to a small fire at the theater, quickly brought under control. However, there was considerable smoke damage and some rubble.

From then on, the Lenox faded from view, eventually to be taken down by the wrecking ball, the location now being occupied by a gas station---an ignominious ending for a once glorious enterprise.

The legend lives on though. As recently as 2005 the N.Y. Times reported on a former North End resident, Fred Cohen, sixty one years old, who announced to his family the year before that he was determined to climb 19,340 ft. African Mount Kilimanjaro, a lifetime dream. Cohen gave as his reason that as a boy he had seen many Tarzan movies at the Lenox featuring the renowned African mountain in the background and vowed to someday climb it. His daughter, Tes, a twenty year old student at Connecticut College, soon signed on. Several months later they made the climb successfully together plus several porters, hiking eight days to the summit. Sadly, Cohen died of cancer, the following year.

The Lenox Theater, Mount Kilimanjaro, Fred Cohen!

Thomas Snell Weaver

High School

1956

Graduation Exercises

Bushnell Memorial Hall

Thursday Evening, June Twenty-first

Nineteen Hundred and Fifty-six

Figure 14

Bad Boys

This chapter could easily be called, "How to flunk high school and still graduate on time" because that pretty much sums up my experience in that so called hallowed institution. From my freshman days at St. Joseph Cathedral High, my school years were a disaster. It wasn't the school, it was all me. I had no ambition, no direction and saw no value in school. In my mind, it was a wasted four years.

While it's true I wore the green corduroy sport jacket and tie required by St. Joe's dress code daily looking every bit the part of a student and showed up for class that was the extent of my involvement. Actually, I could have stayed home the whole four years, Weaver included, and done just as well---as the movie title says "Wake me when it's over." I was bored and not interested in anything but mischief.

Based on the quality of my past school work, I was slotted into a College Preparatory Curriculum, including Algebra I, Latin I, English and Ancient History, being the courses I remember. Since I steadfastly refused to do any homework at all, academic collapse quickly followed, especially in Algebra and Latin that required daily due diligence.

With few exceptions, my ninth grade buddies were of the same ilk: do very little school work, the absolute minimum if possible, and above all do not distinguish yourself, except as a troublemaker. Being a good follower, fooling around and doing nothing became the norm.

When my sophomore year rolled around, I convinced ma to let me transfer to Weaver High. All my friends were making the move, so why not me, too. Upon arrival on the Weaver campus in the fall of 1953, I brought with me an atrocious record of classroom failure in Latin and Algebra—not even borderline grades-- and just barely passing my other subjects.

Weaver didn't think much of my track record—their being an academic powerhouse school--and immediately assigned me a freshman homeroom since I had not earned the necessary credits to be considered a bona fide tenth grader. Moreover, I was demoted to a slow track general course curriculum. Soon, I would be assigned to a bevy of shop classes, General Math, English, and Music Appreciation where I could continue my scholarly descent.

I could have cared less.

The changeover found me enrolled in Mr. Van Schaack's "English for Dummies Class" (*My title)*, or General English class. Better known to his students as "squeaky" for his high pitched voice, it was rumored that our teacher had his voice ruined by a mustard gas attack in the trenches in World War I, allegations probably based on student delusions. Still, he was a veteran faculty member of many years, student newspaper advisor and composer of the song, "Fair Weaver."

There were three things I remember vividly from his class. First, we read a simplified version of Charles Dicken's, *Tale of Two Cities,* my one and only experience with a major work of literature during high school. Images of Madam DeFarge knitting away, the beautiful Lucy Manet and all the terror of the French Revolution even now still flash through my mind, even though at the time I was usually driven to distraction while we studied.

Predictably, some of my same wayward friends from Cathedral—Bobby Murphy, Jimmy Pinto and most likely their cohort, Eddie Buccello--also ended up in that class along with new acquaintances, Dave "carrot top" Kalin and Marshall Davidson. Maybe Harvey Leavitt, too. This gang, a cast of characters, added up to an explosive chemistry waiting to happen. Dave and Marsh, however, were more comedians than delinquents. As I recall, General English was a class of mostly, if not all, boys.

For a while at least, Mr. Van Schaack, well into his sixties and who carried a large black men's umbrella to school—the better to swat butts from the mouths of students sneaking a smoke on school grounds before school started-- distracted us by having each kid read aloud from the text and by allowing Dicken's images to soak into our troubled teen minds. It was definitely the right material for this whacko crew. I remember being totally fascinated and couldn't wait to get to the next chapter.

But, the longer this went on, the more restless the natives got. As these frequent literary encounters with blood, violence and revolution sank in--and, factoring in the arrival of the movie *The Blackboard Jungle* downtown-- our teenage volatility stewed beneath the surface culminating in a classroom revolt; the inmates were loose and only vice principal Ezra "Zeke" Melrose himself would be able to regain control.

As we finished our reading of Dickens, the class became unruly again. The next day someone started a low key taunt of Van Schaack, chanting "O-o-o," then increasing in intensity, as he steamed, until the entire class reached a crescendo, to be repeated unceasingly, despite his pleas for order. That didn't happen, given the insane nature of this crew. The office was summoned and soon Vice Principal Melrose appeared in the doorway looking fit to kill. Just seeing him brought a swift termination of hostilities and we were all sentenced to detention hall after school.

During that time period, a kid named Joe "Red" Dickerson who lived on Homestead Avenue near Edgewood Street, used to host penny ante poker games on his porch during the summer. Bobby Jordan, a big strapping kid, who liked to deal, was fond of offering his own homegrown incantation as he divvied up the cards: *"Take a ride on the poop-ti-do, fella, round and round she goes and where she stops nobody knows."* He was a natural-born dealer.

We were a raucous gang so we didn't last for more than a few days at Dickerson's. After being evicted, we found a new home at Tommy Hogan's house not far away over on Cabot Street where we resumed our games of poker and setback. Of course, being teenage boys, we soon got bored and instead committed ourselves to rounds of strip poker, right down to our jockey shorts. In the end though, ours was a coward's game, and we chickened out before anyone stripped naked.

Hogan was an invalid adult male, confined to a wheel chair, who was very welcoming to neighborhood teens and liberal about what happened around his house. We all liked Tommy, and he loved the company. For a while at least, Cabot Street held our limited attention span enough so that we spent hours digging a hole in the ground for a club house in an empty lot nearby and covering it with planks.

Dickerson, though, was definitely a juvenile delinquent with issues. For reasons I don't recall that year he overdosed on a bottle of aspirin, leading two of our guys, Jordan and Maniznicki, who were close with Joe, to pay him a visit at St. Francis Hospital and spring him from his hospital ward. This was not an unusual action for Dickerson who was constantly getting into trouble and spent a number of his adult years in state prison, where he died in middle age.

Halloween was celebrated throwing barrels off the Sigourney Street Bridge or stealing hubcaps from cars.

Jordan and Claude Paine, both kids a year ahead of me in school—of course almost everyone was ahead of me at this point—started picking me up in Claude's newly bought car at my house for the ride to Weaver mornings. In a time when not every kid had wheels, this valet service made me feel like a king of the road and so important being seen in the company of upper classmen. In truth, however, no one was paying attention.

Hot rod wheels set to go,

Rock 'n' roll on the radio,

Smoked butts, daddy-o,

Sweet little coupe, ole!

Jordan was very strong and gifted athletically. Had he chosen to, he could easily have been at least a two letter man at Weaver (baseball and, football being his fortes), but instead he opted for work after school and cash flow---then enlisted in the U.S. Army without graduating. In our little gang, his physical strength was unsurpassed. For instance as we sauntered up Edgewood Street one evening as per our routine, I remember him lifting Ricky, who weighed about one hundred fifty pounds, over his head horizontally like he was a bar bell. What a fullback he would have made for the Weaver Beavers and how they could have used him in those down years for the football team.

On the other hand, Paine was short and more interested in cars and girls than in school or sports and went on after graduating to a successful career repairing foreign cars.

Evenings, we kept the same monotonous routine. We met up on Sigourney Street between 6:30 and 7 p.m. I raced out of my house after a hurried supper to meet the boys, three blocks away on Sigourney Street. Never did I think about doing homework. From our departure point, we meandered around local neighborhoods, while our court punster, Bernie Scott, who was quick witted, amused us with his latest creations, or didn't depending on our mood. I can still hear Jordan's rebukes: *Did ya stay up late last night, Bernie, thinking that up? Yeah, he practices in front of a mirror, someone else quipped. (We were a band of wise guys!)* King Bernie *was* also a master at ranking on other kids, us included. So user beware.

In the months to come, we made ourselves a home in front of the Lenox Coffee Shop on Albany Avenue, diagonally across from the Lenox Movie Theater, where we would congregate for a nightly ritual of loitering, making contact with Whitey Corbett, the beat cop, who was on foot and showed up to chase us away, followed by our very slow circling of a block or two before returning to ground zero.

It was our hang out, both outside on the corner and inside on the counter stool. As payback, when we were in the money, we'd scoot inside for a cup of coffee, slice of pie, a smoke, or a tune on the juke box. The owners never bothered us much. *They probably wouldn't have dared.*

Over time, we merged with other kids who became more or less regulars with us—Jimmy Pinto, Bobby Murphy, Eddie Buccello, who all worked part time at the filling station across from the Coffee Shop, and sometimes Mike DeFronzo who lived close by, or Harry Barber, a well-known Hartford detective's son. Girls were seldom part of the mix.

Actually the only one who could claim to be a lady's man on the corner in those days was curly-haired Johnny Maznicki, proud owner of wheels early on, and never seemed to be without a girlfriend. The rest of us, as far as I could tell, were celibate. Johnny was a risk taker and didn't think twice about taking some of us for a spin, days before he officially turned sixteen.

Not surprisingly then, when two sexy sounding girls called the public phone outside the Coffee Shop one night and proposed sexual favors of an undefined nature, we were thrown into a teenage sexual frenzy. The girls told us they were from Windsor and invited us to meet them in front of the Plaza Movie Theater there. Without any hesitation, we stampeded in the direction of Paine's car and were soon heading their way. Or so we thought, being all too dumb teenage boys. In Windsor, there wasn't a girl in sight, anywhere, let alone at the Plaza Theater. All too late, we realized the call was bogus and could have come from anywhere, even from Weaver Beaver girls right around the corner and that we had been had, big time.

Night after night, we stood on that same corner, garbed in white T-shirts and dungarees. Smoking came with the territory, almost any brand would do—Chesterfields, Old Golds, Pall Malls, Camels, Lucky Strikes, non filters of course. Bumming cigarettes from other teens was also the norm. To be cool, the sleeve of the T–shirt would be rolled up tightly to use as a place to stash your pack of smokes; single cigarettes got stored behind the ear lobe. Some of our numbers slicked their hair with Vaseline and got D.A (duck's ass) haircuts. I never went to that extreme but opted instead for a Chicago style cut, also popular, which was a modified crewcut on top, D.A. in back look. We liked to punctuate utterances with words like "man" and "cool." Clyde McPhatter and the Domino's, "Mary Had a Baby," a slow bump and grind tune when dancing, were favorites.

That fall I hooked up with Lenny, a kid from Garden Street who was in my frosh homeroom. He got us invited to a party up on Upper Albany—somewhere in the vicinity of Adams, Baltimore/ Milford Streets, can't recall which for certain. I think it was either a birthday or Halloween affair a girl from Weaver was throwing on the top floor of a three family. I sat on the couch next to the hostess who shared her name with me, as I did mine. Not much more passed between us except we quickly melted into each other's arms and made out passionately for the rest of the evening, a typical teenage tryst of sorts. Unfortunately, they were to be few and far between.

Most teens frequented the Lenox Theater, especially on weekends when school was out. Fridays and Sundays were our usual choice of nights. In my case, however, on at least one occasion I hooked up with a different group of boys for a movie, a threesome with nasty reputations. Their favorite pastime was flinging "hawkers" (gobs of spit) onto innocent victims several rows ahead of us, or from the balcony. It was disgusting. And we soon got the Lenox bounce from Mrs. Treske.

These same boys bullied kids at school for lunch money. One poor kid who we referred to as Kung Fu got hit up every day outside the boy's room, especially in cold weather when we were looking to score a hot meal. They would punch him in the arms until he gave in. I never actually participated in these extortion attempts but I was present. In the end, he always paid up and on those days we were well fed and I shared in the bounty. Teen boys can get caught up fast in brainless activity.

By the end of that first term I had become a denizen of the Weaver underworld. Outside of school, I also had a couple of adults attempt to sexually molest me on two separate occasions, in one case, ending in my uncles stepping in to protect me.

In the other one, I found myself nearly trapped inside a local gas station with a mechanic asking me to pull my pants down. I think I was fourteen at the time. Realizing the danger, I fled to the rest room and locked the door, then opened the window and climbed out into the alley and ran all the way home.

But no adult seemed to be able to come to grips with the issue of my pathetic academic record and behavior. My poor mother, Ella, my godmother and probably Uncle Jimmy tried in their own ways but failed.

At Weaver, even though I'd been a decent B student throughout grammar school, my continuing failure didn't cause any alarm. Ezra Melrose, vice principal at Weaver, who had been a friend of my father's growing up, called me in once for a chat but all I remember him wanting to talk about was the good old days. (According to family stories, my dad had once saved his life from an oncoming train. Melrose and dad also had trained together as young men, Ezra as a Trinity football player, dad, an upcoming boxer.) Melrose actually told me he was no match for dad in the ring, though he outweighed him.

My Music Appreciation teacher, Reggie DeVaux, was the sole teacher during my four years of high school who gave me hope. After I wrote an impromptu piece for him on Debussy's *Le Mer,* he began to build up my confidence in his own special way. First, I was moved to a small teacher's desk next to him in front of the class. Almost simultaneously, he rechristened me "Denise." He could be very funny and the following year when my buddy, Michael Angelillo, took his class, he renamed him Michelle.

DeVaux used to write out passes to the Boy's Room for me, even though he knew I was going there to sneak a smoke. He also kept a plastic machine gun that shot water in the coat room and sometimes launched surprise attacks on students. This man, constantly seeking ways to help me grow, was the first to mention the possibility of college for me. He awarded me the only A's I ever achieved throughout high school, and during my subsequent time in the Air Force he stayed in touch, writing to encourage me.

I owe him a lot.

One fellow creature then was a Weaver student with a troubled history who I used to run into outside of school, known as Crazy Sammy, or something like that. Late as usual, I started out for school one especially bitter winter morning and just reaching Platt's Deli on the corner of Magnolia Street, I noticed him fast approaching in a dark blue heavy overcoat, collar upturned. "Hey man, ya got a butt." he inquired. I noticed he was heading away from school. After I gave him a smoke, he hit me with it, snickering: "Let's go downtown and roll some drunks." *It was too early in the morning for this insanity. I shook my head in utter disbelief.* Flabbergasted, I headed off to school while he continued on his way.

This beat went on for the next year and a half. In junior year, however, two things happened that changed the direction of my life. Some of those same nasty kids turned on me and bullied me, psychologically and emotionally, once even threatening physical violence. Their leader, who must have recently been overdosing on Tarzan movies, began calling me Cheeta on the corner and in school and mimicking ape-like itching and chattering. He thought he was pretty comical but not if you were me. Along with his cronies, they turned it into a campaign of harassment. They never missed an opportunity to let loose on me every time we passed in the halls at

Weaver. It seemed everywhere I went, they were lying in wait, for weeks on end.

It was very painful and I grew more and more depressed. At home, there was no one I could talk to about it. To make matters worse, my tormentors convinced others to join in--- some, kids I considered friends. It was my only experience with bullying, and perhaps I was reaping the bitter fruit of my own mistakes of judgment.

The bullying was quickly overshadowed by the talk of a gang war.

The Gang War

It was the strangest of spring times. Waves of teenage angst and rebellion and much public apprehension swept the country after the movie, *The Blackboard Jungle,* and the song, *"Rock Around the Clock"* was released in late March, 1955 and soon opened at Loew's Poli on Main Street. Nationwide, dancing in the aisles, the tearing up of seats and rioting in theaters followed showings in many places. Hartford braced itself for trouble. I recall hearing the words "rumble" and "Daddy-o" for the first time and seeing boys attempt to make weapons out of their belts by wrapping them around their fists. Police officials were calling Rock 'n Roll communist-inspired music.

In May of that year, I was a 16 year old high school junior. After a long day of goofing off at school and working a few hours part time, I would head out immediately after dinner to hang out at the Lenox Coffee Shop at the corner of Lenox Street and Albany Ave, with a motley crew of teenage boys. These usual suspects included Bernie, Bobby J, Claude, Rick, Eddie, Bobby M, Jimmy and Johnny.

Occasionally Harry "the Crooner" Barber showed up to serenade us with his renderings of "Drink, Drink, Drink" from *The Student Prince* movie backed up by the Coffee Shop's jukebox. He did this on multiple occasions, and though he had a splendid voice, I always wondered what drove him, given the hostility from the other kids over his serenading. Yet, no one ever dared mess with him, as he was a hefty football lineman and his father, a Hartford Police Department detective.

Ever since starting high school together, we laid claim to the Lenox Coffee Shop as our turf and home away from home, Whitey, the beat cop, notwithstanding. Our evenings were passed smoking, swearing, taunting, punching and joking. In those days, we still had cops who patrolled Albany Avenue on foot and part of our nightly ritual was hearing him tell us we were loitering, followed by the order to move on. Usually, this led to us simply moving very slowly around the block, then returning to our corner.

All this changed on a night in late April when the phone in the public booth outside rang. The call came from a neighborhood youth widely referred to as "Mad Louie." Louie was being harassed and chased by a group of West Hartford teens and into a public phone booth outside Howard Johnson's on Farmington Avenue, resulting in our mad scramble for cars on a "save Louie" mission. We screeched out of the parking lot and headed west with one stop at Maxwell Drugs at Blue Hills for reinforcements. However, by the time we arrived at the scene of the action, Louie was alone, the source of his troubles now gone which greatly disappointed us.

We imagined that was the end of it. Little did we know that in the next few days, Louie would be busy working the phone lines, issuing challenges for a gang war, pitting Weaver teens against Hall High kids. In fact, word of the "rumble" didn't reach us until after plans had already been set in motion. It was to take place in front of our high school, Weaver, on the night of Inter City Choir practice.

At school, word spread like wildfire. I can still remember hearing kids in the locker room before gym class talking about preparing baseball bats with nails driven through them, car chains, and zip guns to be hidden in Keney Park across the street. Things had gone crazy, but we accepted it in all seriousness. And it never dawned on our limited teenage minds that maybe, just maybe, school and other authorities might have found out.

On the appointed night, I got into a car on Sigourney Street with three other kids heading for the designated field of battle. It was a somber ride—no music, no small talk, no boasting or joking. The silence went unbroken until we reached the traffic light at Albany Avenue and Woodland Street. "Geez, did 'ya see that?" I asked, pointing to several Hartford Police Department squad cars parked curbside showing gas masks and other riot gear in the rear windows. My buddies remained speechless.

Without hesitation, we approached Weaver via Blue Hills Avenue. At Greenfield Street, we spotted fire trucks with hoses out near the south side of the school. Still, no one spoke. This self-imposed moratorium on talk ceased when we were forced to stop at a police roadblock in front of the main doors to Weaver. The policeman asked what we were doing there and we answered "Just out driving around, Officer."

We were pleasantly surprised when they immediately waved us on, especially after the souped up car in front of us sped off, burning rubber, and without halting with cops in hot pursuit. Nevertheless, half a block away, we were pulled over in front of the Emanuel Synagogue. We were ordered out of the car and up against the wall, spread eagle, to be frisked for weapons. The car was also searched, and our names and addresses taken. No arrests were made in our group or any of the others, leading us to believe we had escaped without consequence.

In the following days, it was all over the front pages of the Hartford Times and Courant. One headline: "Gang War Averted." Kids from Hartford, West Hartford, Bloomfield and as far away as Granby, girls and boys, were picked up in the police net. My mother noticed the news coverage and quizzed me about my whereabouts on the night of the gang war. I lied, telling her I was at the Northwest Library Branch hitting the books. *My poor mother---when was I ever studying?*

Not long afterward, detectives from the Hartford Police Department descended on Weaver, setting up an interrogation room in one of the counselor's offices at school. We started being called in individually for further questioning. In reaction, much time was spent in the lunchroom and locker rooms attempting to refine and coordinate our stories to get everyone on the same page. We were bent on survival and a policy of non-cooperation.

It didn't surprise me somehow that the police were seeking information. Both newspapers had gotten a lot of facts wrong about the alleged participants and we assumed the police were misinformed. For starters, Louie was never named as the instigator and ringleader. Other details were badly botched. Two friends, well-known Weaver football players, who had never in the least bit been involved had been mistakenly picked up in the police sweep and gained undeserved attention.

After the police closed shop at school, it seemed the worst was over. However, not for me. In the days that followed, while at my part-time job in the stock room at Seaboard Distributors, my outraged five foot tall godmother, Aunt Ella, suddenly appeared clutching an envelope. She stepped up and slapped me across the face in front of my co-workers. "You're coming home, right now," she ordered. Once inside her brand new white, Cadillac, this diminutive lady who had promised my father on his death bed "to watch over me" informed me of the letter's contents. It was a court order resulting from the night of the aborted gang war ordering me and my co-conspirators to appear in Juvenile Court in June of that year. I was stunned.

For a while, I thought life, as I knew it, had ended. Both my aunt and mother demanded that if called to testify I should tell all I knew and turn state's evidence. In my view, they had seen one too many Hollywood crime movies. "They're my friends. I can't do that," I protested. "I'd have to leave the state." After all was said and done, my line of reasoning prevailed.

When my day in court arrived, I showed up for the hearing accompanied by "my ladies" on both arms. Curiously, the rear of the courtroom was packed with dozens of young men, all wearing white tee shirts who I guessed were our adversaries from Hall High. I was wrong. Instead, it turned out they were the latest class of police cadets assigned here as part of their training. Sitting, up front, we, the accused, formed a large crowd of unhappy boys and even some girls that day, guarded by our parents.

What followed was a harsh tongue lashing by the judge. In addition, we were sentenced to a year of probation to be removed from the records permanently, if successfully completed.

It was.

Champions

Probably the crowning moment of three years at Weaver High was witnessing the two state championships our basketball teams won in the 1954 and 1956 seasons. Previously, no Hartford schoolboy basketball team had ever clinched a title and only one, Weaver in 1945, had made it into the state finals, only to lose to the perennial champion, Hillhouse, 32-28. That squad then was quickly eliminated in the opening round of the New England tourney.

Nevertheless, after over two decades of school history, by the early 1950's at last our basketball teams were vastly improved and a new day was dawning at Weaver. The 1950-1951 quintet logged a 14-2 record, followed by a 14-3 record in 1951-1952, and a 13-6 record in 1952-1953, making post season play in the CIAC State Basketball Tournament possible.

Soft spoken Charlie Horvath, a Silver Star winner for his actions as a Marine Lieutenant on Iwo Jima in World War II, had taken over as coach. Before him, Weaver had suffered through a humiliating twenty four game losing streak. Under his leadership, however, the Weaver program quickly reversed itself and ran up a 67-20 total record overall in his first seasons. Things were looking up for the green. Meanwhile, Northeast Junior High, a prime pipeline leading into Weaver, was busy racking up four consecutive city junior high titles.

For the sake of historical perspective, it is important to keep in mind that the fifties were a time when Weaver High, along with fellow schools in the Capital District Conference (CDC)---New Britain, Norwich, New London, Hartford Public, Bulkeley, and Bristol---were Class A large schools, with Weaver usually weighing in with approximately 1,300 - 1,400 students. The CDC was then a powerful, very competitive group. Such is not the case today when city schools have been divided into smaller units or charter schools.

That summer of 1953, in what was perhaps a harbinger of things to come, Jack Hartfield, Frank "Boo" Perry, Frank Keitt and Ted "Ronnie" Jefferson, all Weaver players, teamed together on a talented Bellevue Square team that captured the coveted Park Department League championship. At the same time, another Weaver teammate, Ron Harris gained experience playing for a Windsor Street squad and, like his other teammates, came back to school in September with renewed confidence.

Even so, when newcomers Cathy Godbout and Marie Tine, future cheerleaders, and Johnny Egan, future Weaver basketball great, stepped on campus as freshmen in the fall of 1953, none of them in their wildest optimism could have imagined what their four years at Weaver would bring, or that they were entering the magical age of Weaver Basketball.

This season was to be like nothing before it. In December, Weaver made an immediate statement by whipping Bristol High 74-58 on the road, Ted Jefferson leading the way with 18 points and Ronnie Harris adding 16. From there, Weaver rolled to a mostly brilliant 19-1 season utilizing their trademark full court press, our only loss coming in the Bristol rematch 61-57 at the Trinity Field House. Weaver also came away with the annual City Series Championship versus HPHS and Bulkeley.

Still, when the CIAC state basketball championships opened in March, undefeated Hillhouse of New Haven, and not Weaver, was the choice of the experts to take the title. Their opinion made some sense because even though Weaver had only lost one regular season game, at times they had played through a number of nights when they had not performed well. Plus Hillhouse had already won nine previous titles, making them the odds on favorites.

In opening round play, Weaver came out firing, dismantling Crosby High 87-60, announcing to all doubters right from the start that we were not to be ignored. After putting up 49 first half points, Weaver went on to total 87 points, the most ever scored in CIAC tourney history. Four starters hit in double figures. Ron Harris led the way with twenty-five points.

From this time on, if not before, some in the north end, began referring to the team as the little Globetrotters, a testament to their deft ball handling skills and court magic.

Together with Weaver, two other Hartford area teams made the quarterfinals---Hartford Public and Hall High. Some had HPHS as the tourney dark horse, as the Owls had impressed with an easy 69-47 opening win over previously unbeaten Stratford---Sonny Thomas scoring twenty-one for the Owls in that one.

Around this time, some Bulkeley High players, after losing a hard fought opening round game to favored Hillhouse 57-49, speculated that Weaver, with its quickness and full court press might then present a challenge for Hillhouse if they were to meet.

For the quarter finals, Weaver got matched against Hall and cruised to a 62-41 victory, setting up a semi-final game with arch rival Bristol, the source of their only loss during the regular season.

Could Weaver beat Bristol? Bristol had previously reached the semi finals fifteen times to Weaver's four appearances. And, Bristol had been to the finals ten times, Weaver only once, possibly stacking the odds against Weaver. But Weaver fans remained confident.

In what was the biggest margin in semi-finals history, Weaver whipped Bristol 76-55, leading at one point by as much as twenty eight points. Weaver played one of its best games to date, highlighted by four of our players scoring in double figures led by Jefferson and Harris. On this night, Weaver probably could've scored 100. I recall joining my fellow jubilant Weaver students shouting "Boston, here we come," as the victory also assured us of being one of the two Connecticut representatives for the New England Schoolboy Tourney.

There was much excitement in the locker rooms and hallways of Weaver and on street corners in the evenings. Although high fives were years into the future, our student body was pumped up.

Meanwhile, top seeded, Hillhouse kept busy routing Roger Ludlowe High of Fairfield, 62-43, winning their twenty fourth straight game and setting up a state championship game versus Weaver before fifty five hundred fans at the old New Haven Arena.

Though the finals were being aired on WATR-Waterbury radio and WHAY New Britain, tickets were being sold at the school, and I wanted to see the game in person. Fortunately, my friend, Claude Pane decided to drive down and along with three other boys I got to go.

Since there were regular fist fights outside some high school games in those days, once in New Haven the walk from the car to the arena was fraught with tension. We banded together, never straying far from our enforcer, big Bob Jordan, a strapping six footer. *After all, we were in Hillhouse territory and could be jumped at any moment, or so we thought in our teen paranoia.*

The atmosphere inside the arena was on fire. Every play was life or death, every shot contested. Amazingly, Weaver steadily embarrassed the physically bigger but slower Academics. In the second quarter, Weaver starters hit on five of eight field goal attempts and managed to out-rebound the bigger Academics. By halftime, Weaver had seized a ten point lead, 34-24 and the Academics, who had given up an average of about thirty nine points in each of the three previous contests, knew they were in trouble. Throughout the second half, Weaver steadily pulled away, shooting an incredible fifty percent from the field, and earning a stunning 58-42 upset victory. In the final moments, I recall Weaver's backcourt tandem put on a bit of show time wizardry that left everyone dazzled. Comparisons with the Harlem Globetrotters were bandied about, on a smaller scale.

Amazingly, Weaver had proven to be better in the state tourney than even the regular season. There were no off nights this time. Sam Bender, the Hillhouse coach, said Weaver was "as good a team as he's ever seen...the fastest." Bigtime compliments from a legendary coach.

It was our first dream season, our first dream team.

Ted Jefferson scored 15 points, Ronnie Harris, 13. Both were named to the all tournament team. Only one Hillhouse player, Harry Bosley with 10, even reached double figures. Overall for the tournament Weaver averaged 70 points a game to opponents 50.

Nonetheless, our celebration was short-lived. The powers-to-be immediately turned around and matched Weaver and Hillhouse in the first round at the old Boston Garden of the New England Schoolboy Tourney. This time, before 11,000 fans, Hillhouse avenged their New Haven state finals loss with a 84-76 victory, in what the Hartford Times termed the "roughest game on record."

It turned out Sam Bender, Academic's coach, had a plan to reverse his team's fortune after his New Haven loss to us. Believing Hillhouse had an advantage on its bench, Bender steered his team into a bruising street ball kind of game. Hold two veteran players out of the starting line up and if possible then get Weaver in foul trouble and wear them down. With two players in reserve, plus a deep bench, he believed he would be sitting pretty.

Unfortunately, he was right. His scheme worked. Weaver, which had viewed the Boston Celtics – N.Y. Knicks game that afternoon, had all it could handle in their own monumental struggle with Hillhouse. Though Harris still hit 20 points and Keitt 15, all five Weaver starters fouled out compared to four for Hillhouse.

Hillhouse prevailed in the highest scoring match in New England High School Tourney history—a total of one hundred sixty points scored. Their eighty-four points were the most single game total ever, and Weaver's seventy-six, the second best all time. A total of 68 fouls were called and an incredible 68 made in a rare show of foul shooting brilliance, both sides hitting 100 percent.

In the battle of the coaches, at least on this night, Bender ruled.

1954---1955

Our 1954-1955 basketball season was a rebuilding, transitional year. Weaver had graduated four of the five starters from the state championship team of the previous March. Only one, Ted Jefferson, returned in the fall, and unexpectedly even he was gone for medical reasons less than a month into the new season. They also entered the new season having the unenviable big target on their backs as reigning state champs.

Henry "Beans" Brown, Jerry Roisman, Dick Reilly and Bob Pollack were the new core of veteran players. But emerging star, sophomore, John Egan returned and fans were also excited over some newly arrived and much heralded members of the sophomore class and winners of the City Junior High Championship at Northeast

Junior High---Bob Countryman, 5'11, Ted McBride, 6'2", Bob Shannon, 6'6", John Harrell, 5'11, and John Sullivan 6'1", a transfer student from the south.

The season opened with an unexpectedly easy win over Windham on the road, 57-41, providing coach Horvath with hope about the season just beginning. In this one Johnny Egan stood out, hitting on a variety of shots from all over the floor.

Optimism from the Windham win didn't last long. A few days later and still on the road, this time before 1,200 at the Bristol State Armory, Bristol High, thirsting to avenge their embarrassing tourney loss to us the previous March, scored a convincing 70-57 win.

Bristol got off to a quick 12-0 lead before Weaver hit their first shot. Controlling the backboards, the bigger Bristol team's lead ballooned to 18-3, then 24 -6 at the end of the first quarter and 37-18 at halftime. Late in the third quarter Bristol still maintained a 51-24 blowout. In the fourth quarter Weaver rallied to cut the lead to nine points at 61-52 with three minutes left but exhausted themselves playing comeback ball, and couldn't pull it out, having built too big a deficit.

Henry Gaski led Bristol with 24 points but sat out much of the second half with four fouls which partially accounts for the Weaver comeback. Ted Jefferson, still on the team at this point, hit for twenty four, Beans Brown had 14 and John Egan,12.

Over a month later after just winning three consecutive games, Weaver met Lou Bazzano's Bulkeley Bulldogs at the Trinity Memorial field House and lost 64-49. This put us in the difficult position of having to win three of four games in order to be eligible for the CIAC State Tournament. Beans Brown with 12, and Vern Lee with fourteen led the way.

Howard Dickerman's Norwich team then crushed Weaver in early February, 82-66, their big center Ralph Dobiejko having his way with us, dominating the back boards and tallying 23 three points. Some fast break baskets helped somewhat to keep us in the game for a while and John Egan made some of his signature long field goals but it was not enough.

The highlight win of the year came in the return match against Bristol, this time at home, in overtime 50-48.

Overall, Weaver suffered a losing season but the inexperienced sophomores who had been given lots of playing time were now veterans, and Coach Horvath was looking to the future.

1955---1956

This could also be known as the season of the juniors, for it was pretty much their team now and Horvath was ready to give them the reins.

Almost as soon as their sophomore season ended, many of this kiddie corps formed the nucleus of a Roxy Diner team in April, 1955, advancing to the late rounds of the Goodwill Boy Club Tourney, honing their hoop skills still further. When summer vacation came around, a powerful Arsenal team that fielded Bob Shannon, Ted McBride, John Harrell, Russ Carter, Bob Countryman, Herb Lewis, Ray Glass, Raleigh Lewis and John Sullivan captured still another Park Department Intermediate Division Championship.

Then in late October, Coach Horvath hosted a Bob Cousy Basketball Clinic at the Weaver Gym, which many area coaches and whole high school teams attended. Red Auerbach and Togo Palazzi also arrived with Cousy. Ten Weaver players helped Cousy out with demonstrations before the hundreds present. Cousy also selected four Weaver kids to run the fast break with him. What a jump start that must have been for a Weaver squad looking ahead to the coming season, and quite possibly one of Coach Horvath's most brilliant moves.

Shortly thereafter, and in conjunction with this event, the buzz at Weaver and on the street corner was that as a result of the exposure he got at the clinic, John Egan was now very much on Bob Cousy's radar, a development that would pay huge benefits for the Branford Street kid's future.

Game two of the season saw Weaver trounce the East Hartford High Hornets 58-37 on the road, in what was a less than stellar effort by the Beavers, all except for the third quarter when they went on an 18-4 run, shooting fifty percent from the field. Egan, with 13 points, (seven straight at one point) topped all scorers, Harrell added 10. Sullivan and McBride ruled the backboards.

In the fourth quarter, the lead ballooned in Weaver's favor to such a degree that Horvath was able to clear his bench for long periods.

A couple of days later on the road against the New London Whalers in a disputed game Weaver emerged on top 71-69 in an overtime thriller. Regulation play had ended in a 65-65 tie. In the overtime, John Sullivan hit his shot giving Weaver the lead. But the Whalers quickly answered knotting the score again at 67-67. Weaver scored taking the lead 69-67. Next John Harrell canned a layup from under the basket, the ball appearing to hit a wire before going in. New London tried to get the hoop disallowed but officials said they did not see the play. After this, Harmon for New London scored making the score 71-69. But, it still wasn't over. With fifteen seconds left, the Whalers got two foul shots but missed both and Weaver then froze the ball. Harrell ended with 22 points, Egan 20, Sullivan, 13.

When Weaver came home to play highly rated Norwich Christmas week, the little Weaver gym was packed with six hundred fans. I remember how much I marveled watching our varsity team warm up and seeing them dunk repeatedly on lay ups. Because of his great spring and large hands, even, Egan, at 5'11," dunked. It was so exciting. It was also amazing to see Egan's deep jump shot, seemingly launched from outer space, earning him the nickname, "space."

On this night, however, Howard Dickerman's Norwich Free Academy team reminded us there was still work to be done. Led by 6'4" Ralph Dobiejko's 23 points, Norwich came out on top 67-61, after falling behind by as much as 50-42 in the third quarter. But early in the fourth quarter, the Wildcats cut the lead down to two and then tied it at 57 all. Weaver ended up losing 67-61 in a hard fought dose of reality with seven lead changes. The loss was especially tough because we led most of the game. Ted McBride scored 13 points.

All three city teams—HPHS, Bulkeley and Weaver---fielded strong teams that year. When City Series play opened in early January with Weaver against Joe Kubachka's Hartford Public five, Weaver was sporting a 6-1 record, Norwich being the only loss. HPHS was defending their city title from the season before. One thousand fans were present at Trinity Memorial Field House to see the battle, with Weaver emerging as winner, 64-55. Like many of these games against the Owls over the years, the outcome was uncertain until very late when a 48-48 tie was broken by Weaver, with 3:35 left, scoring eight straight points. Bob Countryman hit two key free throws. Then, Weaver and Egan froze the ball for a minute. Though Egan stood out with 24 points and for his splendid ball handling and passing, it was a solid team effort. Countryman added 14 points, Sullivan was strong on the boards, as was McBride.

A week later, also at Trinity, Weaver was pitted against Lou Bazzano's highly regarded Bulkeley Bulldogs before 2,400 fans, resulting in a 58-52 win for Weaver. Going into the game, Weaver had not beaten Bulkeley in two years. Once again, Weaver exhibited a strong overall team effort taking advantage of their height and dominating the backboards. The win upped Weaver's record to 2-0 and vaulted us into first place in the City Series. At the three minute mark, John Egan launched one of his incredible long jump shots increasing the lead to ten points at 54-44 with three minutes left. Later on in the month, in the rematch Bulkeley evened the score beating Weaver after we blew a big lead.

Bristol came to town on January 21st and Weaver topped them 59-46 before a small crowd of only five hundred at Trinity Field House. Weaver led by only 48-42 with 3:25 left, shooting a poor twenty five percent for the night. Bristol came on strong at one point in the 4th quarter hitting eight straight points, while holding Weaver scoreless. Lucky for us Scotty Carter's team was struggling through one of its worst seasons, otherwise we might have been in serious trouble. Egan with 17 points and Countryman with 14 led the way.

Early in February, Weaver, now 11-2, hosted a New Britain team in a game that turned into another Weaver sub-par performance on our home court. Some of our poor play came from not having John Sullivan available due to illness. Without him, it was nip and tuck down until the final two minutes and New Britain actually led 24-18 at the half and were ahead still by 32-26 in the third quarter. Then Weaver went on a 12 point run, taking the lead 38-32. Before the game ended, it was knotted at 40-40 late. However, Weaver pulled away 55-48 with two minutes left.

Days later Hartford High, (7-6) and smarting from the earlier loss to us, whipped us soundly 69-51 before 2,000 fans. The still-sick John Sullivan was not available, reducing Weaver in size and inside game mostly to outside shooting and allowing big George

Zalucki to go off for 25 points. Though Weaver's inside game was hurting, we managed to stay close in the first half but Hartford High pulled away in the second half and led by 23 points with 3:30 left. Egan with 23 and Harrell with 14 points, mostly long range, led Weaver which shot a lowly 25 percent from the field.

It was a year when we just couldn't seem to figure Howard Dickerman's Norwich team out. On the road in the second match, and what turned out to be the finale against the Wildcats, Weaver lost 76-70 and in doing so lost the Capital District Conference (CDC) title. Norwich led throughout: 22-12, first quarter; 44-33, halftime; 57-52, third quarter; and 60-58 with four minutes to play. Even with John Sullivan back in the line up and scoring 20 points, Ralph Dobiejko, with 27 points, and company, proved once again to be too much for Weaver. Egan chipped in with 18 points.

So entering the CIAC Class A Tournament, Weaver had now lost the City Series title to a three way tie and also the CDC championship. We were 12-5 but Norwich was 12-1 and powerhouse Hillhouse was undefeated. So much for Weaver, it would seem. Nevertheless, we had won two years before and we were more than ready.

When the CDC All Star team was announced in March, two Norwich players and three Hartford area players were named: Weaver's Johnny Egan, Hartford Public's George Zalucki and Bulkeley's Joe Reilly. Ted McBride from Weaver was named to the second team.

Weaver opened tourney play with an uninspiring win over Stamford, 67-64, making us 13-5.

In the quarter finals, sixth ranked Weaver was paired against defending champion, undefeated top seeded Hillhouse before 4,500 at the New Haven Arena which practically served as the Academics alternate home court, being an Elm City school. Undaunted by this challenge and energized by John Sullivan's 17 points and John Egan's 15, Weaver managed to stay even in the first half, then steadily pulled away from Hillhouse in the second half for a 59-51 win. Weaver fans went bonkers relishing our second CIAC tourney win over Hillhouse in three years.

With Hillhouse out of the way, the road to the state title was now wide open.

Weaver next drew Fairfield Prep in the semi finals and drubbed them, 75-58. In this one, Egan set a single game tourney scoring record, hitting 29 points. Harrell chipped in with 14, McBride, 12 points. We were now 15-6 and feeling good.

The championship game in 1956 was an all Greater Hartford final: Weaver vs a tall Manchester quintet, a 65-52 battle with Weaver coming out on top, though Manchester had been favored, largely because of their superior size. Manchester came out smoking and shot an unbelievable close to 50 percent from the field in the first half. Seemingly unperturbed, Weaver stayed close and only trailed by five points at halftime. Fast breaking, pressing, Weaver went on a 22-6 run to open the second half while holding Manchester scoreless until there was 1:45 left in the third quarter. Also, the Indians got into foul trouble. With 3:30 left in the game, Weaver led by 15 points and began slowing down the pace. In the end, John Egan had the ball at center court, dribbling like the All American he was becoming, as time expired. Russ "Skeeter" Carter played a major role in the victory especially with his ball hawking style defense. John Egan, John Sullivan, Bob Countryman, Ted McBride all sparked a great team effort. Weaver had shot an impressive 22 for 33 at the foul line, though field goal production was a low 25 percent.

John Egan scored 18 points, setting a new tournament record for most points scored, 62 in the final three games. He also was named tourney MVP and unanimously selected to the all tournament team. Ted McBride made second team, while John Sullivan and John Harrell received honorable mention. Al Cole of Manchester scored 25 points.

We were going to the New Englands for the third time---1945, 1954, and now 1956--- and Boston fever quickly set in. Even for a non-student student like me it became impossible to concentrate in class. Very quickly we learned our opponent in the first round of New England Tournament play would be the Maine state champs, Morse High from the town of Bath. Almost as soon, I learned my friend Dave "carrot top" Kalin and Marshall Davidson were planning to drive up for the game and they invited me to join them, along with Ellen Yush and Sandy, a girl whose last name I can't recall, there being several Sandys in our senior class.

I recall on the ride up we all had good laughs berating the "oafs" from the woods of Maine, the potato pickers who didn't stand a chance. How wrong we were.

Starting two 6'4" players and a well-rounded team, Morse crushed Weaver, 78-57. They were simply too big and too fast. Following several lead changes, Morse led 36-29 at the half and 57-50 at the end of the third quarter. Weaver then floundered scoring only seven points in the critical fourth quarter. We pressed in vain. Morse had five players in double figures and shot 47 percent---a great team effort. Weaver, on the other hand, shot only 30 percent from the floor. Egan had 18 points but no one else for us reached double figures.

Hartford and the Weaver student body showed our immense pride in our team and officially recognized their achievements at a school assembly in April. On behalf of the business community, Max Savitt, the lawyer, presented each member of the championship team with reversible Weaver jackets. His brother, Bill, gave the cheerleaders compacts.

Almost immediately, began the dreams of next season dancing in our heads when Weaver would return almost the entire starting five as seniors.

1956---1957

Greatly encouraged by how well they had done, most of the returning veterans: co-captains, Egan and Countryman, McBride, Shannon and Sullivan challenged themselves that summer by teaming together on the same Park Department squad at Keney Park, coached by Walter "Doc" Hurley, and stepping up a level to the senior division, although their ages made them eligible to play in, and in all probability, dominate the lower junior division. They didn't win the league but they got oh so much better going into the new season.

This was to be a Weaver basketball season for the ages in which they would capture the City, Capital District Conference (CDC), Connecticut Interscholastic Athletic Conference (CIAC, Class A) and New England Interscholastic Athletic Association (NEIAA) titles, all the while remaining undefeated 24-0 throughout, the only loss coming to our own very talented alumni team late in December and that only by two points and not counted as an official game.

Russ "Skeeter" Carter stepped up early replacing John Harrell, who had graduated, on the starting five, joining with Egan, Countryman, McBride and Sullivan. Carl Littman proved ready for the sixth man role off the bench along with 6'6" Bob Shannon. It would be a year of "blinding speed, deft ball handling, and tremendous shooting," as lauded by the staff of the 1957 Weaver yearbook. Add to that a tenacious, pressing defense and you had the makings of a championship caliber squad.

The season commenced facing the usual December foes--- Windham at home, followed by East Hartford on the fourteenth of the month. East Hartford proved no match allowing Weaver to an easy 74-50, twenty four point victory. Egan went off for 18 points, even though not playing in the fourth quarter. McBride added 13 and Countryman, 12. Weaver was up 15 points at the half, 38-23. Coach Horvath emptied his bench for the final quarter. The team shot a solid 40 percent from the floor. Leo Mazzoli shined for the Hornets, putting in 19 points.

Nearing Christmas, Weaver and New Britain High clashed before 1,000 at the Central Connecticut Teachers College Gym. In what had to be considered an atypical performance, Weaver hit on only six field goals in the first half. Moreover, John Egan, saddled with four fouls, scored a lowly two points, something that had never occurred since becoming a starter. How would Weaver respond without production from "Space"? The answer came loud and clear from Ted McBride and Russ Carter who stepped up, combining for 21 and 20 points respectively and allowing Weaver to come away with a 62-53 victory. John Sullivan added 12, helping spearhead the effort.

At the end of December, Weaver, playing before a frenzied home crowd of 746 (some fans actually being turned away at the door), stomped the usually tough New London Whalers, 72-33, McBride with 15, Egan 14 (ten in the 3rd period), and Sullivan 12, led the way, benefiting from the fine passing of Russ Carter. Overall, Weaver shot 50 percent for the night and headed into the new year with a perfect 6-0 record, four of the wins coming in important CDC league competition.

The start of the New Year brought an always strong Scotty Carter Bristol High quintet to the Weaver gym. A partisan crowd of 500 watched a stiff battle, with Weaver emerging on top, this time 61-53, proving the CDC one tough league. Weaver's usually reliable full court press failed them on this night, and with Bristol still hanging around late in the contest, Horvath was forced to go to a freeze in the last minutes. Countryman, McBride and Sullivan were strong on the boards, but McBride did sprain an ankle. Egan netted 22 points, Sullivan 13, and Carter 10.

On January 25th, Weaver met Lou Bazzano's Bulkeley Bulldogs in front of 2,000 fans at Trinity Memorial Field House, the usual site for City Series games. Surprisingly, Weaver rolled to a 72-52 win, highlighted by great Weaver defense and a dazzling 22-6 run in the first quarter when they hit on 10 of 12 field goal attempts. In another great team effort four Beavers hit double figures: Egan, with 22, Sullivan, 16, Countryman, 12, and Carter, 10. The team hit on 43 percent of their field goals.

Six days later, before a capacity home crowd of 700, Weaver tangled with New Britain High for the second time earning a 66-59 hard fought win. This time Skeeter Carter, with a career high 25, and Bob Countryman with 19, took over the scoring duties while John Egan sat, hobbled by four personals.

In mid February with the season winding down, Weaver journeyed to East Hartford for the rematch with the Hornets, drawing 1,600, including many from the north end. Following a slow start, Weaver took over the backboards and started running their fast break, opening a a 34-18 halftime lead. By the end of the third quarter, fueled by its relentless press, Weaver increased the lead to 45-27, leaving little doubt as to the outcome which would be be a 63-41 Weaver win. The effort lifted Weaver to a 17-0 record, thus becoming the first Hartford team ever to go undefeated in regular season play.

Weaver got to the CIAC tourney that year as the only undefeated team in the tournament at 17-0. In their first game in New Haven, they knocked off Hamden High 60-40 on a slippery Arena floor, sending a signal to all comers that the green were not to be denied. Next up was an always strong and fast Wilbur Cross five who we topped 68-60.

For the semi finals, Weaver overcame Bridgeport Harding 73-64 before 4,500 fans. In first half action, Weaver shot the ball poorly and it was up to always dynamic Russ Carter to step up and keep us in the game, scoring a career high 16 points, ending with 18 for the night. Harding attempted to stop our fast break but got into foul trouble. The early stages saw many lead changes but it was 24-21 in Harding's favor at the end of the first period. In the second quarter, Weaver's press kicked in and caused Harding trouble, during which we shot 50 percent and took the lead, 27-24. We ran the lead up to 51-48 in the third period, off a 14-4 Weaver run. We then slipped into a semi stall at the start of the fourth quarter, John Egan putting on a dazzling ball handling show. Egan came away with 22 points for the night, a brilliant 16 from the foul line out of 17 attempts. Countryman and Littman, plus two Harding players fouled out. Although Harding shot a decent 66 percent from the foul stripe, they lacked the overall firepower necessary to win.

We now had our ticket to the New England Interscholastic Championship at the Boston Garden for the fourth time in our history (1945, 1954, 1956 and 1957).

First things first. There was still the matter of a state CIAC Class A basketball title to be decided and who better to battle than our old nemesis, the Hillhouse Academics of New Haven, our third meeting with them in four years. As we entered the final round, Weaver became only the fifth team ever to arrive undefeated in both regular season and tournament play. Unlike the earlier, less attended games, 6,000 fans showed up for the Championship.

Weaver led throughout, in a closely contested match, ahead 40-31 at halftime, after out rebounding Hillhouse 12 to 4 in the second quarter, but losing ground to 53-52 in the third period, then allowing them to take a short lived one point lead. However, Egan proved too much in the fourth quarter scoring 18 points himself. At 3:01, Weaver went into a partial slow down but it was only after John Sullivan hit a crucial hoop with 1:50 remaining, increasing the lead to 69-64 that Weaver fans breathed easier. In the end, it was up to jumping jack, Skeeter Carter to kill the clock dribbling at half court. Weaver had prevailed 77-72.

Ted McBride scored 16 points, Sullivan 15. In a category of his own, Egan broke the single game tourney scoring record with 33 points, making 13 of 17 foul shots. Giving it his all, Bob Countryman fouled out for Weaver. In a brilliant performance for the Academics, Ken Tullo came away with 31 points, and not to be undone 15 of 16 foul shots. Both Egan and Sullivan were selected to the All State first team, and Bob Countryman and Russ Carter made second team All State.

Egan and Tullo, Weaver and Hillhouse would soon meet again.

A big bake sale was organized for March 10, 1957 at Weaver to raise hundreds of dollars needed to help defray the cost of the team's trip to Boston, some of the baked creations divvied up by the players who made short shrift of their prizes.

Bigger prizes lay ahead. At 21-0, Weaver was riding the crest of the greatest season of school and Hartford high school basketball history. And, of course, as if everyone didn't know it already, they soon would: we had John "Space" Egan, arguably the best schoolboy player in New England and no one else did. We also had a very balanced, very experienced squad.

In a little known pre-tourney move, Weaver coach, Charley Horvath invited the other Hartford high school head coaches, Bulkeley's Lou Bazzano and Hartford Public's Joe Kubachka to assist him in Boston. They accepted, immediately providing Weaver with the benefit of their many years coaching experience.

The stage was set and Weaver was more than ready.

During this time, I was far off deeply immersed in USAF basic training in Texas where mail call brought whole issues of the Hartford Times with news of the team's progress from my sister, Eileen, then a Weaver freshman. I hungrily devoured each copy and shared with several other Connecticut airman basics. In my barracks, everyone was soon rooting for Weaver.

In the first round, Weaver rolled over LaSalle High from Rhode Island, 75-59.

Wasting no time, on the very next night, there was a return engagement with Hillhouse. It seemed there was always a second time around against the Academics, this time attended by a disappointing crowd of 7,562. Inspired by our own great defense---Hillhouse was held to a lowly 26 percent on this night and Tullo was scoreless in the first half--- Weaver grabbed an early lead and pretty much kept it. In the effort, three Hillhouse players accumulated four personals. Weaver led 17-15, 27-20 at the half, 45-38 and 56-47 with 3:15 left. Egan hit 7 of 7 from the foul line, the team 18 of 26.

Next up was the battle of high school titans, Weaver, now 23-0 versus New England Catholic School Champion, Lawrence Central Catholic at 27-0, the monumental contest of the undefeated. And, if this was a season for the ages, this was the game for the ages.

And, on this night 11,000 fans were on hand. The game came off nip and tuck with many lead changes throughout. With seven seconds left Central had taken a 64-62 lead and had possession of the ball under their own basket. In a great defensive play, Ted McBride somehow managed to deflect the inbounds pass to Egan who then was fouled. Following a timeout and with everyone in the Garden standing, and with four seconds remaining on the clock, Johnny calmly sank both free throws, tying the game. The crowd went wild.

In overtime, Weaver hit eight straight points and went up 70-64 in the first forty seconds of play, throwing Lawrence Central completely off balance. Further, Central was now being harassed everywhere, resulting in steals for Weaver. By dominating the overtime, Weaver won the game, 85-73 and the City of Hartford had its first New England title. Our team had scored an amazing 21 points in the overtime, Central 9. Egan alone outscored Central 12-9. There was the splendid defense led by Bob Countryman and Russ Carter, plus the rebounding of Ted McBride and John Sullivan that helped tip the game but the performance everyone present would remember forever was that of John "Space" Egan who topped all scorers with 36 points, including thirteen field goals, an incredible 32 of them coming in the second half and overtime sessions. One of the finest performances by a high school player ever, as declared by the Providence College Friars and many others as the "best high school player in New England."

The unassuming days of boyhood when Johnny could be heard pounding the ball up Branford Street for hours of hoops on the Keney Park playground court with pal Lenny Schoolnick, and others from the hood---Bobby Pollack, Carlton Hodges, Mouse Waterhouse, Vic Pugliese, to name a few--- were not yet over, but numbered. Soon, Weaver and the north end would have to share him with Providence College, then the NBA and the wider basketball world.

THE 1956-1957 WEAVER NEW ENGLAND INTERSCHOLASTIC BASKETBALL CHAMPIONS: Bob Shannon, John Sullivan, Carl Littman, John Egan, Russ Carter, Bob Countryman, Ted McBride, Jerry Falvey, Stan Goodman, Rick Turner, Dave Bovitz, Ben Thomas, John Noman, and Raleigh Lewis and of course, Coach Charley Horvath.

The Light

My life started improving further during the summer leading into my senior year at Weaver. Still, even though the gang war was history, the bullying lingered. And, on top of everything else, I lost my part time job at Seaboard Distributors. It felt like I had hit bottom.

Whether it was the weight of the judge's probationary sentence following the aborted gang war or a growing maturity I can't say, but I grew increasingly anxious to put this all behind. Step one in my plan for a new life was to seek out new friends. In my mind, hanging out at the Lenox Coffee Shop had ceased to be an option.

It's not quite clear how this happened, but one night I just walked away from the Coffee Shop, never to return.

From then on, instead of bolting out my front door every night for Lenox Street, I set my sights on Maxwell Drug Store, three quarters of a mile to the west on the Avenue to the corner with Blue Hills and a whole new set of kids, initially little known to me.

For my new nightly routine I would cross over to the north side of Albany Avenue at the corner with Vine and the historic landmark of the Horace Bushnell Church on one side, the legendary Jack's Pharmacy on the other, then in quick time scoot by the old Stop and Shop at Sigourney Street, across from the Spinning Wheel Restaurant.

Much of Albany was residential at this point for a block or two, but there was a mixed use, commercial-residential block on the other side where my older friend and recent Weaver grad, Frank D'Addio, an albino who was good with the numbers and a lover of the game of chess, could be seen working at Frank's Edgewood Luncheonette. In the same block, my Weaver buddy, Richie McGill, voted the boy with the cutest nose in the senior class, had just finished up his part time job stocking shelves at the very small First National Store. A block later, I strolled right by the Lenox Coffee Shop, slowing only to see if Murphy, Pinto or Buccello, corner acquaintances, were out pumping gas at the Shell station, across the street at Cabot. And who could miss the Lenox Theater right next door, where on a given night Tommy Shea, another classmate, was busy popping corn for Mrs. Treske.

As I passed Sterling Street, I soon put McCarthy's Pharmacy, a popular spot with kids, behind me on the south side of the Avenue. Then it was on one more block to Woodland but not before giving a wave to Harvey Leavitt, another Weaver senior, laboring at the Woodland Garage on the other side. Harvey smiled back; Harvey always seemed to have a smile.

From the corner with Woodland, I loped the remaining few hundred feet by Northwest-Jones Junior High grounds, quickly reaching the front doors to the Hartford Public Library Northwest Branch, which I sometimes frequented. The remaining distance being negligible, I slowed my pace. Across the street Mott's Super Market loomed.

At around seven, I walked over to Maxwell Drugs and took up space along the black, iron railing on the west side of the building almost directly across from the Dairy Queen, there to be greeted by Carlton "Hodgi" Hodges and Bobby "Digger" DiGregorio, the regulars. Very quickly, I fell into lighting up a smoke, or bumming one.

Across Blue Hills to the other corner, we could see Weaver's Marty McGuire busy pumping gas for his after school part time gig at the Amoco station with the red, white and blue sign and the torch. The north end and downtown Hartford provided a lot of part time jobs for teens back then.

Much to my surprise, since my changeover to this new hangout, I had blended effortlessly in with the Maxwell's regulars. In fact, it was almost miraculous how quickly it happened, as if my time at the Lenox Coffee Shop had never taken place.

Soon we were joined by Anna Minelli, who lived around the corner on Harrison Street, and Martha Reardon who lived a long way off further up Blue Hills, two friends and classmates at Mt. St. Joseph Academy in West Hartford---Mounties. Anna, Martha, Carlton and Bobby were longtime friends, from earlier times at Keney Park.

The block Maxwell's was on included the Baggish Bakery, the Blue Hills Deli and a branch of Society for Savings. The store was much larger than the typical corner pharmacy of the 1950's and contained a long lunch counter and booths to eat in among its amenities, a magnet for teens. It saw a lot of foot and car traffic.

As one of the regulars, albeit a newcomer, this would be my new home away from home. As I grew acclimated to the Maxwell's scene, I learned we were not the first generation of kids hanging out there. And from time to time "alumni" happened by. Guys like Victor Kravitz, Mike Sullivan, Louie Pugliese, the Kellihers. There were also young bloods like well-known kids simply called "Sponge" and "Mouse." There were also old timers like Russ Noyes, or Mr. Noyes to us, a Hartford firefighter and a huge Johnny Egan fan.

When I think about it now, the usual night there probably passed uneventfully, perhaps even insipidly. I recall musing that somehow our nights resembled a scene from a Marty Chayefsky play from those times like "Marty." *What do you feel like doing, Marty? I don't know what do you feel like doing? We outta be doing something.* Many the night I had that feeling.

Little did I know then that these corners had some interesting history. Where Maxwells stood, McGurk's Blacksmith Shop existed, fifty years before. Across the street where the Amoco Gas Station was located, at the turn of the twentieth century and for many years before it there was the rambling Adams Inn in the age preceding automobiles. Finally, over on the other side of the Avenue close to Milford Street land was occupied by the Hartford Fair Grounds (in later times, the Gentlemen's Driving Park), going all the way back to the 1850's and where in May of 1861 the Third Regiment of Colt's Rifles were encamped prior to deployment in the Civil War.

Most excitement resulted from the beat cops chasing us away from the corner, probably at the behest of Maxwell Drugs and other nearby establishments who I'm sure couldn't have been too happy about our continued presence.

Other times the sight of Big Jack pulling his car up to the curb brought excitement. At these times, we anticipated the possibility of driving around with Jack at the wheel, provided he hadn't already arranged to chauffeur any Weaver athletes, his first priority, especially Johnny Egan and Lenny Schoolnick and in times before them Mario Sottile.

An unforgettable local character, Jack was a large, single man in his late thirties, somewhat childlike, who worked at a local warehouse and lived at home with his mother. He was top heavy and possessed very spindly, weak ankles, forcing him to always wear sneakers. Oftentimes, the poor guy was prone to flatulence. If we were inside his car when this happened—Jack seldom left his car-- windows opened, fingers went to noses, hands and arms would gyrate wildly, kids would scream, "Jack… ARRGH!" Jack would wiggle uncomfortably in his seat and smile.

As he did with us, he would chauffeur Weaver athletes around town and sometimes older guys, home from college on their dates. Being slow of wit, of course, he was subject to teen cruelty and ridicule. In one incident some kids actually borrowed his car, drove it, and then returned it with a wrecked transmission. On another occasion some of the older guys set Jack, who was a virgin, up with a local nurse who was turning tricks on the side. When asked afterward how it felt, his answer, "Kinda tight," resulted in much laughter.

The corner was not always quiet. In fact four years earlier, a crew of teens had witnessed an 18 year old youth named Foran knocked through Maxwell's plate glass window severing a vein, all over insults hurled at a 15 year old girl the week before. The two culprits made their escape by Connecticut Company bus to Portland Street close to downtown. Foran's friends eventually located the accused and were about to launch a revenge attack when a beat cop saw this and corralled the wanted kids, preempting an attack, but not without difficulty.

Nothing of this sort occurred during my time on the corner. There were moments of local color though. Mad Louie of gang war infamy showed up one night, just as a young boy pulled his bicycle up to Maxwell's, parked it outside and then ventured inside. Since no one locked bikes in those days, Louie seized it, opened the front doors to Maxwells and rode the kid's bike up and down the aisles, exiting with the druggist chasing in hot pursuit. Mad Louie really was mad.

As that summer and fall progressed, others joined us: Mary Fitzgerald, Rose Fazio, Joey Fradianni, Frank Rondinone, Santos (Sal) Stylle and his cousin Gus Nicholson, a recent Weaver graduate. There were some who stopped by occasionally --- Victor Pugliese, George Mercadante, Ralph Callucci, Gil Slocum.

Such a good group of kids. Carlton, a.k.a. Hodgi, was an upbeat, classy kid, the point guard for a strong Hartford Jewish Center basketball team. Bobby, a.k.a .Digger, was a witty, recent Weaver grad, now attending the old UCONN Branch on Asylum Avenue, across from Hartford College for Women. We became good friends.

They could also be a very funny duo. Girls with large breasts who ambled by, for instance, were "Umm, ripe on the bough, mon-- scrumptious." Hodgi liked to do Louie Armstrong imitations and carried a handkerchief to mimic one of the jazz great's signature moves with his horn. The first time I recall Hodgi doing this was after a viewing of *High Society* at the Lenox Theater. The three of us were ambling along near Woodland and Albany when he treated us to an impromptu version of "And That's Jazz" from that movie. They also liked to conjure up the weirdest names of NFL players, some real, some of their own invention, one that still comes to mind—the fictional, Bibbles Bobbles.

I can still see our whole gang working its way up Blue Hills Avenue, heading nowhere in particular, bantering as we went, Joey Fradianni getting kidded about his fixation on Rose Fazio with her immediately firing back: "Tell him to come back when he grows up." Poor Joey, being Weaver's football captain got him little romantic yardage.

Some nights Gus and Santos busied themselves in bouts of "Greek style" arm wrestling in the small grassy area alongside the Maxwell's block, with no declared winner, their being cousins.

Santos' father owned the Wonder Diner on Albany Avenue and both he and Gus lived on Irving Street, the latter two houses from me. Their families were originally from the Island of Cyprus. Both owned cars and enjoyed driving around town. Gus, who had graduated from Weaver that June, liked to chase girls. Santos, who was in my homeroom at school liked to drag race and sought out drags on North Main Street with me riding shotgun. We found them, sometimes they found us.

I remember one night Digger, Hodgi, Martha, Anna and I think maybe Emilia Mascaro and I walked all the way to Martha's house on West Euclid Street to play something called "Doink" on her enclosed front porch. I only remember its name and at one point having to squeeze our noses during it, an innocent enough parlor game.

I had a midnight curfew in those days and West Euclid was a couple of miles from home so upon leaving I found myself in a jogging race home with Digger and Hodgi, completely winded, but getting in under the wire, then having to get up and drag myself to school the next day.

At still other times, I found myself in the company of Richie McGill, who was quite popular with the girls, and stopping by house parties in the Blue Hills neighborhood. Rich and I would continue our friendship in our United States Air Force years and beyond.

On cold nights, or sometimes not, we'd venture into Maxwell's, take up seats at the lunch counter and order a piece of pie, in my case blueberry, a cup of coffee, a cherry coke or a lime rickey, and light up a smoke, all for practically nothing. A cup of coffee then was fifteen cents, a plain coke, ten cents, add another two cents if it was a cherry coke. Pie was a quarter or so. Always short on cash, if there was a need, we helped each other pay.

Some nights a band of us, girls and boys, would pile into Big Jack's car in front of Maxwell's and just sit there gabbing. Other nights we'd go for a ride---one of the more memorable ones, a joyride on Deercliff Road in West Hartford, known for its challenging contour, especially when exceeding the speed limit. More often than not, Jack would give us a ride home, right to our door. He was a good hearted guy.

These newfound friends were a godsend for me after my previous hard times at the Lenox Coffee Shop corner, making me feel optimistic entering my senior year at Weaver while still lacking in academic goals.

Just before school resumed in the fall, I landed a new part-time job at Brown Thompson & Co. on Main Street in the Paint and Wallpaper Department as a combination sales clerk and stock boy, a position I would keep for the next year and half until entering the Air Force. My boss was Bill Waxgiser, in his late twenties, a graduate of the University of Miami and a recent veteran of the Korean War. His assistant was Mrs. Elizabeth Gray, a wonderful, matronly woman from an old West Hartford family whose husband worked at the YMCA.

Bill was very boyish looking and handsome. His father owned a large paint and wallpaper operation in Stratford and the location in BT's basement was a franchise. Almost as soon as arriving in Hartford to manage it, Bill catapulted to a position as one of the city's most desired bachelors. Young women were constantly stopping by the department, looking for attention. Witnessing the parade of admirers, Mrs. Gray would simply roll her eyes and smile. Other times after they left she would feign a swoon and moan, "Oh, Billy, Billy!"

This employment was perfect for me. In addition to the grunt work stocking, I got to interact with customers and make sales which I found really gratifying. Moreover, Bill became like a big brother to me and a very important male figure. He seldom treated me like a subordinate and he and Mrs. Gray were playful and friendly; they always treated me like family. Mrs. Gray even let us call her Betty, which I usually passed on, deferring to her age.

By nature boyish, Bill liked to have some playtime. He would call me out back to the stock room to shoot hoops using rolled up paper and a wastebasket, intensely competitive sessions. None of this ever detracted from the job. We played and worked but not necessarily in that order.

Bill also watched out for me. When he noticed another man, a suspected pervert, employed by BT's, taking an inappropriate interest in me, he cautioned me to stay away from him and warned the guy to leave me alone. What a positive influence as was Mrs. Gray!

In October, I rode to East Hartford in Harvey Leavitt's 1930's makeover auto for our football team's game with the Hornets of East Hartford High. Kalin and Davidson and probably Arnie were along. There must have been someone else, too, because the car was packed. Following the game, another Weaver loss, as we drove back we noticed a couple of girls walking along the road leading away from the school. It turned out they were Weaver girls— sophomores—who the guys recognized and offered a ride. Given the crowded conditions, a girl named Chickie ended up sitting on my lap.

This led to my first official date. Chickie was very attractive, the Alan Freed Halloween Show was coming to the State Theater and I wanted to go. I phoned and asked her out. She accepted. I was so thrilled.

We doubled with Tommy Radigan, a recent Weaver grad and the former catcher on my Jay Cee Courant League baseball team. He had a car, I didn't. It was that simple. His date was a cute Weaver cheerleader.

The State was the city's legendary theater, dating back to 1926, located on Village Street downhill from Main. Boasting a wide marquee to be better seen up the hill, it sat nearly 4,000. Almost everyone who was anyone in show business appeared there over its lifetime, except for Elvis who was considered too explosive by management.

Alan Freed was nationally known for his "Rock'n Roll Party" on WINS Radio, New York City. Just the month before in September of 1955, he had broke all records bringing his show to the Brooklyn and New York Paramount Theaters.

The Halloween Show we saw featured Freed, Lillian Briggs, Sam (the Man) Taylor, Happy Brown, El Dorados, Cadillacs, Moonglows, Harptones, Solitairs, Al Sears and the Valentines, hard to believe in today's world but all on one bill.

I recall wearing a vest and blue suede shoes for my date and bopping down Village Street trying to look cool.

The atmosphere inside was electric. The crowd was predominantly young. Up in the men's room, I noticed boys with D.A. haircuts and pegged pants were belting down drinks from pints of whiskey smuggled inside to avoid the police presence. Even before Freed came on, things were getting wild with lots of clapping, foot stomping and screaming.

Remember before this time period, teens were used to a steady diet of Doris Day, Johnnie Ray, Eddie Fisher, Frankie Laine, Dorothy Collins and Snookie Lanson on "Your Hit Parade" and Montavani, or essentially white music. We were ready for a change. Freed's shows helped usher in a new age.

During the show, which was a combination of rhythm and blues and rock 'n roll music acts, members of the audience attempted to get up on the stage and dance with the performers. Police were summoned and some of these kids scuffled with them. At other times, performers came down into the aisles further stirring the crowd. Meanwhile, Chickie, my date got up on her seat and started gyrating.

Celebrating Halloween, the Valentine's came on wearing masks and the crowd kept on yelling for them to take them off, much to Freed's delight. Everyone was going wild---performers and crowd.

October 30, 1955 – Rock'n Roll history was made in Hartford that night.

Afterward we went out to a more staid setting, Lincoln Dairy on North Main Street for refreshments and socializing. When the girls left us briefly for the Ladies Room, Tommy leaned forward with a smirk on his face and asked, "Where did you find her?"

It was my first and only date with Chickie. But I do remember that several years later, this same girl was a semi-finalist as Miss Connecticut in the Miss U.S.A. pageant.

Around this same time, without warning, Red Kalin and Marsh Davidson, those two merry pranksters of the 1950's, announced they were forming a club at the old Hartford Jewish Center on Asylum Avenue. My fading memory presents two versions of this story: one was these guys with their whacky sense of humor wanted the Shamrocks as the name, as a brazen sign of teen irreverence for the host organization, the Jewish Center.

I remember at least a discussion of that name at the founding meeting on the top floor of the Center. And clearly we did have a heavy non Jewish membership: Lowndes, Egan, Murray, McGill, Fradianni, Rondinone, Hodges, Sullivan, meshed with Milstein, Kalin, Davidson, Leavitt, Schoolnick and Arnie Miller.

The other possibility for our name was the Gems, a name that shows up on the back of a 1956 class photo given to me and leads me to guess that at some point, either in the application for approval process or during our discussion during the formation meeting the name Shamrocks was rejected, in favor of the more neutral, Gems.

Much clearer to me was a Weaver female student quite innocently stopping by to say hello and the room being suddenly plunged into total darkness, however briefly, the girl soon departing flushed.

Our club, which was pretty much a sport's frat, was very strong in every sport we played—basketball, touch football and softball. Johnny Egan quarterbacked our football team for which I was a 130 pound tackle. In basketball, three or four of our guys made the Center's All Star Team that played against teams from New Haven and Bridgeport.

The club's founding fathers, Marsh and Red were in their glory.

That fall we heard about some Weaver athletes engaging in a "sport" they called "depantsing". An inductee, always some boy, was picked up by car, quickly deprived of his pants, then to be dropped off outside the home of a girl while the culprits leaned heavily on the car horn. They would then drive off leaving their prey cowering in the bushes and not knowing when he would be rescued.

On Thanksgiving morning, I rode a crowded bus of Weaver supporters to Wethersfield Avenue for the annual HPHS-Weaver football battle. Weaver lost as usual.

Not so with basketball. Even though the previous season was lack luster, because we returned a strong nucleus of juniors, our basketball team looked more promising. Every home game was packed full with the Weaver student body and City Series games versus Bulkeley and HPHS at Trinity Fieldhouse drew thousands. Our team was led by future Providence College and NBA star Johnny "space" Egan, a kid who could make shots from so far away they seemed to rain down from outer space.

Our wildest dreams were realized when our team—16-4 entering the tourney—beat favorite Hillhouse High of New Haven early in the tournament and went on to win the State high School title for the second time in three years. Then, it was on to the New England schoolboy championship at the Boston Garden.

Everyone was so excited. Dave Kalin, Marsh Davidson, Ellen Yush, Sandy, (whose last name I can't recall there having been several Sandys in the Class of 1956) and I drove to Boston to support our team against a strong Maine team, Morse High of Bath, just as they had pitted another good Weaver team in 1945 against another team from up north. I still remember us making light of them as a team of "potato pickers" from the sticks. They were no country yokels on the basketball court, though, and Morse crushed us 78-57.

Tragedy struck that February. Jimmy Pinto, 18, a senior at Weaver, crashed his car into a utility pole in a Blue Hill's neighborhood with two teen passengers, one his 14 year old brother, a Weaver freshman, Lou, who died from his injuries at the hospital. There was also a 15 year old girl present who survived. The whole school went into deep shock and mourning.

Throughout that spring, another Weaver senior, Tom Schiponi, made a name playing "Cherry Pink and Apple Blossom White" on the trumpet at assemblies and prom night, so much so it could've been considered our anthem. My date for the prom was a Bulkeley High girl and sorority member named Joyce. We doubled with Ray Smith, a friend from home room, who took a girl from Avon. So we drove all over the place before getting there. It was a very hot night and the Weaver gym, site of the Prom, was sweltering. I was drenched.

Somehow I graduated on time, age 17. It had to be a social promotion as I was no student and ranked almost at the bottom of my class. But the passing grade then was a 50, or E and my average was in the low 50's. Whoever at the Board of Education responsible for creating that policy should have gotten an F grade.

The summer of 1956 I expanded my work hours at B.T.'s and played a lot of softball at Keney Park. Every time I got a phone call it was from Red or Marsh letting me know there was a game that day. All the Shamrocks/Gems gang showed and some new faces were recruited—Richie Reilly and Dave Murray, and Eddie Kane, our West Hartford buddy, for starters. I hated playing the outfield at Diamond #2 with its right field gully. I remember Reilly in particular, a lefty, lofting one over my head into the road behind me. Thankfully, I found I was better at softball than baseball, maybe because of the size of the ball (I could actually catch it barehanded and get hits, too). We continued these games until guys drifted away to college, the military and work, late in the summer.

Suddenly high school was over.

Into the Wild Blue

It was an incredible three days. On New Year's Eve Day, 1956, our beloved Cathedral of St. Joseph on Farmington Avenue was destroyed by fire. Even outside my house one mile away, we could easily see the smoke shooting hundreds of feet in the air, prompting my high school friend, Richie McGill—home on leave from the Air Force-- and I to immediately drive there to see for ourselves. Across the street from the scene, we joined a horrified crowd of onlookers in front of Aetna Life Insurance Company.

The destruction of my childhood spiritual home was chilling. Memories of First Confession, First Communion, Confirmation, countless Sunday and other masses, May celebrations of the Blessed Virgin, numerous processions and practice sessions— Catholic education being firmly rooted in practicing—flashed through my mind. Our beautiful, gothic Cathedral engulfed in flames, never to return.

In a bizarre twist that same day, the Hartford Courant headlined a story about St. Patrick's Church in downtown Hartford, my father and mother's childhood place of worship and schooling, being ravaged by fire the day before the Cathedral fire. The photo accompanying the article depicted ice covered ruins, it being bitterly cold the night of the fire. This plus the Cathedral fire started a spate of rumors which never led anywhere about possible church arsons.

That same evening, even with all the sadness and tragedy of the day, we gathered at my grandmother's for a family party to celebrate New Year's 1957 and my imminent departure for United States Air Force basic training. I brought with my hi-fi record player and some current 45 rpm singles to dance to. I remember Jim

Lowe's "Green Door" captivated everyone, getting a lot of plays. Surprisingly because of their differences in age, the guest of honor, my buddy, Richie McGill, 18, hit it off big with my 14 year old cousin, Maureen, and they danced the night away. Maureen's father, uncle Jim, took a liking to Richie and seemed delighted by this development. Aunt Ella Russo, as always, arrived triumphantly and to much laughter, this year dressed as the New Year's baby, diaper and all with a sash across her chest heralding "1957." Ella Russo, an aunt for the ages.

Two days later on December 2nd, I flew out of New Haven in early evening, on a nondescript government chartered turbo prop packed with new recruits, destination Kelly AFB, San Antonio, Texas and three months worth of basic training.

The flight down was not uneventful. There was a forced stopover in Memphis because of engine troubles, grounding us for an hour or two. No one seemed to think twice about it and before long we were in the air again. Over Oklahoma in the early morning hours, we ran into a thunder storm with lightning practically on our wing tips.. The flight quickly turned rough and many of the guys had need of the "burp bags" being handed out by the flight attendant. The resulting sounds of misery and nauseating smells were overwhelming and I had all I could do to keep from gagging. When we finally landed at Kelly Field, our destination, I was shaky but unscathed.

We were lined up on the flight line and someone came and marched us awkwardly to a nearby chow hall. Even though it was about 4 a.m. and few were hungry after the unsettling flight, the prevailing wisdom seemed to be we had a long morning ahead and probably would not have another chance to eat until noon time. So like all good recruits, we accepted our fate.

The chow hall was empty because of the early hour, and we quickly moved through the line. The main course was something called S.O.S. (shit on a shingle, or creamed beef on toast), which I had never heard of before. It looked totally disgusting. And, my stomach was currently in a fragile condition; I rejected it and instead piled two bananas on my tray, afterward making my way to a table. My choice was a lucky one since within minutes someone was calling us to "fall in," military lingo for getting in correct formation prior to marching somewhere.

Later we managed a disorderly march to nearby Lackland Air Force Base and assigned the first floor of a two story wood frame white barracks. There would be no immediate repose, however. Somewhere along the line we got divided up into what the USAF called a "flight," or a squad of twenty to thirty guys, all of ours from Connecticut.

The rest of that day, in fact the rest of the week was a blur of activity. We were marched here and there, from early morning to evening chow time. Soon, we learned to chant "roads guards out" when marching, both day and night, while a couple of our guys swung Air Force issued flashlights paving the way on the roads. We also found out we were still individuals of a sort but part of a "flight," flights being part of a squadron. Our leader was given the title "T.I.," for training instructor, usually a good old southern boy who didn't much like Yankees from New England like us.

Days were filled with activity--- being shorn of most of our hair, being issued g.i. clothing, or uniforms, being corralled through a factory-like line while USAF medical personnel discharged vaccine guns into our arms multiple times---some victims, fainting and collapsing onto the floor. We tried the art of marching, polishing our shoes and properly caring for our living space. This entailed being taught to spit shine our shoes and cap visors, make a white collar bed acceptable to superiors, proper personal hygiene and how to pass inspection at any time of day or night. It was a busy day beginning at dawn and ending at nine o'clock lights out.

We swept our barracks floor using our shoe brushes and buffed this same floor with our g.i. issued blankets, pulled squadron guard duty, once even in pouring rain,, and were awakened at 3 a.m. some days to pull long hours of k.p. duty (kitchen patrol).

Chow and Mail call were the major daily events we lived for. Irving Street and the north end were miles away physically but never far off in heart and mind. In the days when long distance phone calls were still very expensive, letters from home were eagerly awaited. And my mother and sister seldom disappointed in this regard. Letters came, I purchased stationery at the base PX to write my replies. Late in my time at Lackland, through a packet of Hartford Times sport's pages sent from home, I was able to share my jubilation at reading of my Weaver High going totally undefeated for the season, and winning the New England schoolboy basketball championship. My fellow Connecticut basic trainees were amazed.

K.p. was a long work, tedious day from early morning until after the late afternoon meal. I found out early on it was best to arrive early so as to avoid being assigned the more unpleasant jobs, for instance, pots and pans which involved laboring over huge USAF utensils, scrubbing and washing for hours over boiling hot war, in the end hopefully resulting in the approval of the NCO in charge. The earlier the better to land a preferred job like being a server on the chow line itself.

One of my stints was on garbage duty with another guy. The work, smelly but not especially hard, was done outside on an elevated loading dock in the rear of the chow hall. It was a treat just to be outside for something other than marching and I looked forward to a day of this.

The euphoria of the great outdoors didn't last. Not long into it, a flight of newly arrived female basics entered our sight line being marched by their T.I. who was a woman NCO. We hadn't seen a woman for some weeks so our natural response was to wave and yell, hoping to draw their attention. It did. The result of our endeavor was seeing this entire flight of forty or so women make a detour and head in our direction. Stupid us, we were thrilled.

As soon as the flight halted in front of us, their NCO T.I. turned into a raging Nazi storm trooper, glaring at us, calling us to attention. We were stunned and snapped to immediately. She proceeded to rip us up and down in front of her charges. The women watched in silence. In the end she concluded her dissection of us with a dagger, "Garbage patrol, indeed. Well, they got the right boys for that."

The flight of female left us in unison to a chorus of a high soprano "1-2-3-4." We never saw them again but wished we had. Women were scarce during basic, WAFS (Women's Air Force) being far fewer than their male counterparts in the 1950's and were also verboten, or off limits, like the red light districts of San Antonio, to male recruits.

Lackland Air Force Base was large enough to have its own bakery on base and my flight was next assigned k.p. duty there. This would be a singular event since the Air Force liked to spread this escape from regular k.p., endured every three or four days, around.

Knowing this, we quickly fell into a state of heightened anticipation the night before with fantasies of the sweetest kind.

We arrived in pre-dawn darkness after a longer march than usual, the bakery not being nearby. I remember the building as being about the size of an average chow hall. But what I remember most was how a few of our guys were immediately assigned jobs as sprayers These basics were handed what looked like DDT, hand pumped spray guns and ordered to attack the cockroaches swarming on the bakery walls. They had to do this all day, non-stop.

This development got our attention, as did the insect invasion. We soon noticed that the creatures had overwhelmed all such efforts to exterminate them and routinely dropped into cake and pie batter with no effort made to remove them from the baking process. Later that day, when I got a close up look at some pastries I couldn't help but notice the presence of cockroaches cooked in them.

I never took pastry for dessert again while at Lackland AFB.

That same time, there was also an incident at the Bakery that sticks in my mind. A kid from another flight assigned to pots and pans duty was working furiously in scalding hot water when a Mexican American NCO cook—the Air Force in Texas had an inordinate number of Mexican cooks-- appeared and started chewing him out for getting behind. Things got out of control and the cook ended up splashing some very hot water on the airman. Several of us witnessed the incident and came to the kid's defense, arguing with and chiding the man who had staff sergeant rank. He backed off but we didn't. So much for military authority. Our little protest group filed a written complaint against him and heard week's later the man suffered a demotion in rank over the matter. Big doings for guys who were basically at the mercy of these same people.

During the first month at Lackland, I ran into Ed Drydol, my schoolboy friend from Sargeant Street, Hartford and discovered he was billeted near me, having arrived in basic a short time after me. The only other time I saw him was on a day when his entire flight was confined to barracks for some minor infraction—T.I.'s liked to do that—and we were forced to talk through a screen door. Before I left, I got him a soda from an outdoor soda machine and slipped it to him. Not long afterward, he shipped out to tech school for electronics in Biloxi, Mississippi

A few weeks into basic training, our T.I. announced that nearby San Antonio was hosting a Catholic festival including a parade. Any Catholic airman was invited to march, even the newest recruits. I eagerly signed up because I was interested in a getting a look at the city. Those of us who went that day gave our shoes and hat visors an extra coat of spit polish first. We were bused on Air Force blue buses and strangely took a route through what must have been an Off Limits section of San Antonio (there were several) because we soon happened upon a street lined with all naked women hanging out their front doors waving as we passed. If I didn't already, now I knew I was a long way from the north end.

South Texas weather in winter was nothing like in the north end of Hartford. There were occasional cold days and nights but mostly I remember it as being hot with almost no shade outdoors, resulting from an absence of trees. Not long into basic, salt pills were made available to us for the heat. There were also unsubstantiated rumors of something being added to our diet to suppress sexual appetite, which made some of the fellas cringe. It rained a couple of times in my three months there and there was a tornado threat toward the end of basic. If a tornado hit, we were advised to lay on the barracks floor which struck us as absurd since these were WWII era wooden structures without basements. Still, I suppose lying on the floor would have been as good a place to undergo death by tornado as any. Anyway, no one said Air Force logic was sound.

Air Force basic training was run like a Boy Scout camp. One of the supposed highlights was something called bivouac and the obstacle course so there was much excitement when we received word that our time had arrived for a go at it. Since bivouac supposedly meant camping out in the open without tents or cover, we were told to pack up our duffle bags which we did and were marched off the morning in question to a field opposite the obstacle course, in light rain. Upon arrival at the site, we were ordered to pile up our bags, which we did. The T.I. then asked for a couple of volunteers to stay with our stuff. Two of us got the nod, me being one. The rest then left us to crawl and climb around in the rain. Meanwhile, we arranged the duffle bags like a cave, slipped inside and dropped off for a good snooze, it still being an early Texas morning. Later on when the rest of our flight returned, it was announced that bivouacking was cancelled because of inclement weather.

Figure 15: Larson Air Force Base

More proof of the Boy Scout nature of things showed up in P.E., or physical exercise. While we did occasionally visit a vacant field to do calisthenics, these sessions were few and far between. Instead, and incredibly, we got to go bowling and horseback riding. I swear the only time in my life I have ever been on a horse was during basic training. It was baffling. Finally, nearly three years later while reading the Seattle Intelligencer newspaper at my desk in the public information office of my permanent base, I came upon an article that shed light on this very issue. According these news reports, the base commander was undergoing investigation in a kick back corruption scheme involving his receiving lumps of cash from local proprietors of companies servicing Air Force physical training. I never heard further how the case was resolved but I can only assume it couldn't have been good for the top brass.

By March I had developed a nice tan from the many hours marching outdoors. Half of our guys had already shipped out to technical schools for more training. The remainder of us remained to finish out three months in basic, then to be shipped to permanent bases for OJT, on the job training--- in my case because, my lack of academic achievement in high school didn't serve me well on USAF

173

achievement tests. In the last days of basic, we were given seven hour passes off base to San Antonio. We used it to do the tourist thing, visiting the Alamo which was quite disappointing for it smallness and some of us shelled out a few bucks to have a local Mexican American girl, working in a family photo business, in a sultry dress pose with each of us. San Antonio then still had a 19th century quality to it with many older buildings, not unlike many western cities in the fifties. We were also issued shorter on-base freedoms— enough time to catch a current movie at the base theater for a quarter and swig some beer at an outdoor venue. We were winding down.

Almost as suddenly as it started it was over. Lists were posted with information about where we were being shipped and what our career field (AFSC) would be. Larson AFB in Moses Lake, Washington was to be my new home where I would be trained as a clerk typist. We were also awarded our first stripe, making me an Airman Third Class, earning seventy eight dollars monthly. (approximately six hundred fifty 2015 dollars, adjusted for inflation). Finally, we were issued a thirty day leave plus travel pay to our home and then to my new base..

With my new buddy, Kevin McCarthy, a young married guy from New York City, and wanting to save money, I caught a Trailway's Bus out of San Antonio heading north, proudly garbed in USAF uniforms and occupying seats in the second row. In the middle of the next night while traveling through North Carolina a young, attractive local woman named Sue May boarded our bus and sat in the seat directly ahead of us, which was in the first row. The three of us got caught up bantering and flirting and when Kevin nodded off I moved up front with her and soon what had been mostly words evolved into a full fledged make out session that continued all the way into Lumberton, her destination, much to the bus driver's amusement. I never saw her again but what a night to remember.

Life in the north end was far less exciting than my trip homeward, mostly spent visiting family and hanging out with friends back on the old corner at Maxwell Drugs. While home, I did look up my next destination, Washington state, in the encyclopedia and viewing photos with spectacular vistas--- mountains, lakes forests and lots of greenery, leaving me convinced that I was being sent to a virtual paradise. However, no information showed up for a place called Moses Lake.

At the end of my leave, I again traveled by bus, this time because I wanted to see the country, being eighteen years old and not having traveled much. This time there would be no flirtations or on-bus passion. No such luck. It was just me traveling alone on buses that seemed to make stops in every small town across the country for three plus days but seeming much longer.

I remember Denver the most from that first cross country trip for its nineteenth century pre-urban renewal character with many older structures still intact. After that, we made stops at bus stations in a couple real cattle towns in Wyoming, before making the final leg of my journey. The next day we rolled into Walla Walla, Washington, home to Washington State Penitentiary and once a fur trading post on the road to the Oregon Trail.

We were told anyone looking to travel on to Moses Lake and other points west, that it was time to transfer, which we did. Our new mode of transportation was a small van, quite unusual in those days. I never before heard of a major bus company employing anything like it. Three or four of us climbed on board. Not long afterward, the sky up ahead turned very dark, though it was only mid-afternoon. Our progress slowed considerably as we crept forward into a wind-swept storm in which visibility was reduced to nothing. It got so intense, our driver said he was going to make a detour, then swinging miles out of his way in order to circumvent the storm.

In early evening darkness with lots of tumult—sagebrush and tumbleweed careening up and down the main drag—we arrived in Moses Lake. It was like something out of a Peter Bogdanovich black and white production. I thought I it was Moses Hell.

Without difficulty, I carted myself and my duffle bag onto an Air Force shuttle bus for the ride to the base which was seven miles outside town. An off duty airman riding with me and returning to the base, hearing I was newly reporting for duty, mused, "Moses Lake has a girl behind every tree but there weren't any trees." True enough, since the area was mostly flat, dry farm country, hosting several small lakes—Moses and Soap being a couple of nearby ones. I also heard from the same man that Moses Lake was also variously known as "Moses Gulch" or "Moses Hole" to the troops.

The base itself was a former World War II facility now housing a fighter squadron and the 62nd Air Transport Wing for C-124 cargo planes. While Larson was remote, it was considered quite desirable by Air Force standards, mainly for its excellent flying weather; the eastern part of Washington being arid with little rain or snow fall, and, unlike the better known Washington coastline to the west and McChord AFB in Tacoma which was more prone to fog and bad weather.

At this point, I was in a state of culture shock. *I might as well have been on Mars. And I'm going to be here for almost four years, kept running through my head.*

Instead, Eastern Washington and Moses Lake turned out to be a godsend. In this land of tumbleweed, sagebrush, rattlesnakes and large summer wildfires, I underwent a spiritual reawakening and started my formal education in earnest. In my years there I also advanced from a clerk typist in the base housing office to becoming editor of the base newspaper in my final two years. When I departed the Air Force in 1960, I brought home with me a full semester's worth of transferable college credits, having earned them through Washington State University and Central Washington College evening extensions on the base, half paid for courtesy of the USAF.

Unlike high school, my four years in the Air Force were rewarding beyond anything I had imagined and I am forever grateful to the following people from those years: Airmen: Torrington's Hank Pernal, former roommate, Bob Howieson, a farm boy from Mapleton, Minnesota; California's Vern Korschinski whose family was in the election machine business; Ed Tynan Jr., son of a Pittsburgh steel corporation's vice president; New York's Dick Weick, John Stigelmeier, a native of Munich, Germany; Ken Prey, a Florida kid, Andy Davis from Vernon, Connecticut and Latrobe, Pennsylvania's Dick Byers; Sergeants: Peter DelVecchio, Leslie Carpenter, Carl Hassinger and Frank "Pappy" Collins, who had served in the U.S. Army in Central America in the 1920's; Major: Bob Jones, a B-29 pilot in the Pacific War and briefly my roommate; Captains: Amy Jo Smith and Eugene Hungerford; and, finally, Fr. Francis Elliott, base Catholic Chaplain, and June Thompson from Springfield, our office secretary.

And during my Air Force years, I fell in love for the first time with Connie "Cookie" Sapia, a seventeen year old north end girl. I was nineteen.

I received my college letter of acceptance during mail call in late 1960 and proudly showed it around my workplace. On schedule, in December of 1960 I received my honorable discharge and departed Larson with my letter of acceptance into the University of Hartford, inviting me into the School of Arts and Science for the fall of 1961.

However, before heading east and home, I first took a bus bound for Tacoma, Washington and McChord AFB, where two of my good friends, Ed and Vern, had been transferred the year before. Not knowing whether we'd ever meet again, I wanted to see them one last time and stayed with them a couple of days.

Little did I know that while I was there visiting a massive snowstorm hit the northeast and that a civilian airliner had crashed killing its occupants. Unfortunately, my family in Hartford somehow came to believe incorrectly that I would be flying home following my discharge and assumed the worst—in their imaginations, I was flying home on board that plane. Panic-stricken they even phoned Larson AFB and the American Red Cross.

Totally unaware of any of this, completely out of touch, I boarded a train heading east and made a stopover in Helena, Montana for a short a brief visit with Margaret Sullivan, my grandfather's sister, an elderly spinster whom I knew I'd never see again. After an overnight there, I caught another Great Northern train for home, arriving a couple of days later, quite safely, and to much jubilation among family and friends.

I immediately settled into my old room and began life on Irving Street again as a civilian.

Exodus

Figure 16: Irving Street Scene 1961

After the holidays at the end of 1960 and after settling into civilian life, I set out looking for work in the bitterly cruel January of the New Year, one of the coldest on record. I needed full time employment until college started up in the fall. Fortunately, I was quickly hired in the fledgling computer department at Connecticut Mutual Life Insurance Co. on Garden Street, walking distance from my house. There, I would feed IBM cards into a machine eight hours a day, boring but financially rewarding, earning about one hundred dollars a week (eight hundred 2015 dollars, adjusted for inflation), a far cry from the measly, little over a hundred a month during my final days in the Air Force. My mother was pleased by the extra income.

The steady income my job provided allowed me to purchase a black, 1955 Ford, standard transmission, my first car. As events would show, I would own it less than a year.

When fall arrived, I sought part time work, as I was a full time student, first briefly as a Fuller Brush salesman (Brook Street, Sisson Avenue, Park Street territories), door to door, then working at the Hartford Public Library downtown for a more steady paycheck. I was hardly at the library two weeks when Aetna Life responded to a recent job application and interview of mine (Applicants then could still walk into Personnel Departments of local companies without an appointment), offering me a position on their late afternoon "Housewife's Shift" in the Data Processing Department.

I could get in approximately thirty hours a week, running IBM machines, and there was bonus for running more than one at the same time. Sometimes, I could make thirty five to fifty dollars weekly, decent part time pay in 1961. Summers and vacations I would get full time work. And it turned out there was another University of Hartford student, Ed Zajac already working there, someone to pass the time with, making the transition smoother. Ed, a Bulkeley High graduate, had recently returned from military service like me.

My bosses at Aetna proved sympathetic to student employees and around exam time each year I could sometimes study on the job. Naturally at the time of my interview I didn't know this but I eagerly accepted the position anyway. Ironically, Aetna was right across from where my new parish church, the Cathedral of St. Joseph, was rising from the ashes of the fire, adjoined by my former grammar school, putting me back in my old schoolboy territory.

Like a work-study program, Aetna employed me until the late summer of 1964 when I resigned to begin student teaching at Suffield High School. Ed Zajac was there a similar length of time. Aetna made it possible for us to get our college degrees while living at home, sparing us the expense of dorm life somewhere else. Many University of Hartford students lived at home in Hartford then and annual yearbooks reflected that fact by listing graduates local street addresses.

Figure 17: Aunt Ella center with maracas

That fall of my freshman year (1961) was marred by a sad family event on Irving Street. My aunt and godmother, Ella Russo, the heart and soul of my mother's family who had been residing in the beautifully renovated third floor attic apartment of our house for a decade, had been ailing for several months from severe heart complications.

She was relatively young and trim, in her mid-fifties but heart disease had caused her to retain too much fluid in her legs. By summer, they had become so painful that she was reduced to climbing the stairs to her apartment by sitting, then lifting herself to the next step repeatedly until she reached her apartment door. When even that became too torturous, she coped by sleeping on my Noni's couch next door.

By early fall, her doctors were urging open-heart surgery, which was then in its infancy, at Yale-New Haven Hospital. First, however, her overall condition had to be improved which required lots of rest. Gaylord, a convalescent home in Wallingford, was selected for this and she moved there in October.

Around Halloween, we were amused, but not surprised, to read of her adventures there in the New Haven Register and to hear of them first hand when we visited. In the press, she was renamed "Auntie Ella," that colorful female patient who visited the Children's Ward, trick or treating carrying packets of goodies to the kids in her wheelchair. She also played nocturnal games with the staff, one night pulling her sheet over her head and turning on a smuggled in flashlight moaning "O-o-o-o," totally spooking out her nurse while earning herself a reputation for mischief. The same aunt who promised my father on his deathbed to watch out for me.

In December, she was moved to Yale-New Haven Hospital for open-heart surgery. Our family waited anxiously for word of the outcome and finally heard she had survived the operation but was not expected to live. Ma, my sister, Aunt Amy and Cousin Jerome piled into my black 1955 Ford and we rushed to New Haven to see her one last time.

I don't think I'll ever forget the sight of her in recovery, hooked up to life support. It was only the briefest of visits as they only let us into the room for a couple of minutes at most. But it was long enough to form a lasting impression. Not having ever seen anyone in this situation, I remember thinking she resembled a research monkey being experimented on because of all the wires and hoses running into my poor godmother. She died the next day.

Returning to Hartford that day on the Merritt Parkway turned out to be precarious. Not far from Wallingford, we hit an ice storm and I soon found myself trying to keep us from sliding completely out of control. I managed but not without trepidation. It was my first time as a driver navigating on a sheet of ice and left me with a healthy respect for ice on the roadways.

Ella was waked at Laraia and Sagarino's on Washington Street. My grandmother, Lillian, practically collapsed, dropping at the coffin into a semi keening state, "O dia, o dia." Someone in the family even took snapshots of Ella in the coffin. My cousins and I served as pallbearers and she was buried at Mount St. Benedict Cemetery.

It was a difficult Christmas. There would no longer be any Auntie Ella Christmas party, Santa Claus or New Year's baby. Our aunt was gone.

Almost immediately, relatives started bickering over the fate of her material possessions, which were considerable. There was the white 1957 Cadillac, a mink stole, antiques, jewelry, a cottage at Black Point, some cash and land in the North Meadows. At her wake, I recall a relative standing behind me in line waiting to pay his respects saying "How much did she leave us?" Greed was in the air and she wasn't long in the ground before others were putting pressure on Nonni to let them into my aunt's apartment. My grandmother answered by putting a padlock on Ella's door.

While there was no will, there was a letter written the year of her death while at Gaylord and given to me for safekeeping. She knew the odds of her surviving the operation were not good. In it, she seemed to anticipate the direction things would take once she was gone. She wrote: "Now Dennis, they've got to listen to this before any one fights. Only the girls are to be present, all six of them."

Among the stipulations of the letter: Uncle Sam was to get her white Cadillac if, in exchange, he was willing to give his 1955 Mercury to me, and I in turn give my Ford to his daughter, my Cousin Claudia. Ella's sisters received various incidentals, including a diamond ring, mink stole, china, furniture, rugs and silverware.

"The house at the beach will go to all the girls and they will have a vacation each..." she advised somewhat naively which immediately resulted in hurt feelings in some family members, because being the grand manipulator she could be, they had been led to believe the cottage would be exclusively theirs. And, as if anticipating this would happen, she cautioned: "if any one fights, you are ruled out." Uncle Sam Testa and I were placed in charge.

Curiously, no mention in the letter was made of the lucrative fourteen acres of land she owned in Hartford's North Meadow, future home to Superior Springs and the Meadows Bowling Alley and land the Russo Bros. Construction Company, uncle Joe's cousins, bitterly coveted and considered theirs. Eventually, however, the sale of this property resulted in thousands of dollars of income to each of my mother and her sisters.

In the end of her instructions she suggested: "one day... go on a good drunk on me." Would that they had, perhaps there would have been less family consternation after hearing her wishes. Like her mother before her, she liked to manipulate relatives to do her will, in her case by promising things to individuals that in the end would not be delivered. But, finally her better nature seemed to prevail, and she made an attempt to be fair to all nevertheless, leaving some with hurt feelings. It was a dubious legacy.

My aunt's death only added to a steady rate of attrition through death in the neighborhood that harkened back to the end of World War II: old man Winter, two doors over; both my grandfathers; my own father; Charles Morris, next door; my aunt Margaret; Mrs. Johnson, Junior's mom; Tootsie's mom; Hertzel's aunt. And soon, my aunt Vera and I were summoned to the second floor rental apartment of my grandmother's house to verify the passing of our neighbor, Charlie Schlicker, lying dead of heart attack on his bathroom floor. The losses seemed endless.

For some, Irving Street was just a brief stopover on their way somewhere else. The late 1940's and early 1950's ushered in a lot of this. Rose Yush remarried and with son Eddie moved away. The Kahns and Solomons also pulled up stakes. My aunt Peggy got an apartment in East Hartford. The Morris family departed after Charlie died. The changes were small at first but then accelerated as the 1950's wore on.

By the time the 1960's arrived, our neighborhood gradually started coming unhinged. A number of bizarre characters and incidents replaced some of the old families and stability. Petty crime was on the rise, if not on our street itself which was still considered safe, but in the surrounding neighborhoods. Adding to the changing landscape, the wholesale destruction of the eastside downtown through urban renewal forced people and an army of rats our way.

The decade kicked off with excitement though, especially among Catholics over the election of John Kennedy to the presidency. We were riding high. In my own case, I had returned home from the Air Force buoyed by a renewal of my faith brought on by four year's inspiration from friends who either had previously been or were soon to be bound for Catholic Universities (Seattle University, Notre Dame, Loyolla).

So when JFK, as we all called him, gave his famous inaugural speech on that frigid January day in 1961, I was glued to the television set. (The year before, my future wife to be, Barbara Tracy, then fourteen, a member of Youth for Kennedy, was photographed in the crowd standing near the podium wearing her fake straw campaign hat, when Kennedy had made a campaign stop at the Hartford Times Portico.) It was such an exciting time.

Our euphoria was quickly dampened by the Bay of Pigs Invasion, followed by the Cuban Missile Crisis. Fear swept the country. Bomb shelters were being built locally. Air raid sirens were placed at the corner of Garden Street and Albany Avenue and were tested out on a regular basis. We received civil defense instructions in the mail on what to do in case of attack. Incredibly, I had a place toward the back of our cellar staked out in my mind as if we could somehow survive a nuclear attack: megatons of multiple payloads descending on us and me shrinking under an old kitchen table there. It became hard not to reconsider the advice given us in grammar school by the good nuns, "Any time you hear a plane fly over, make the sign of the cross," meaning of course it could be a Russian bomber. Little did we know then how close we came to the unthinkable actually happening.

My big fear was that I would be called back to active service. I was in my early twenties, gung ho, and still considered by the military to be in the inactive reserves as part of my six year overall commitment. It didn't happen but the possibility weighed on me.

Another longer lasting fear came from the unparalleled crime wave that hit Upper Albany. There was nothing new about petty crime in the area, present right from its beginnings as the Homestead Park Corporation at the turn of the twentieth century. Burglary, minor arsons, petty theft and assaults made the police blotters in every decade. But what we started seeing in the late 1950's represented something new in my lifetime.

Among the first cases in the summer of 1959 was a home invasion by a cat burglar in the early morning hours in a Magnolia Street first floor apartment--the victims a family named Grasso, well-known to my sister because one of their daughters, Josie, was a sorority sister at Weaver High. Apparently, adding humor to the Incident, the family dog slept through the break in. It was no laughing matter, however, when the family awoke to find one hundred dollars, a large sum in those days, missing from Mr. Grasso's wallet.

Approximately five years later this same family suffered another encounter with a criminal, this time a peeping Tom who was noticed outside their daughter's bedroom windows. The seemingly fearless Grasso sisters gave chase and cornered him near the corner with

Mather until police arrived. They were subsequently warned of the wisdom, or lack thereof, of their taking action.

In the nights that followed, my sister thought she heard someone outside her bedroom window. Our roomer at the time, John, a University of Hartford Art School student and future FBI agent and I, both wielding baseball bats, searched the area, without finding anyone.

"Strange things" were indeed happening, as actor-comedian Red Buttons sang.

Throughout the early sixties, a steady stream of pocketbook snatching, stolen purses, car thefts, fires, solicitations, hold ups and domestic cases invaded the area. One teen boy was sent to Cheshire Reformatory after robbing two newsboys of their earnings. A drunken neighbor crashed his car into a telephone pole near our house. And as I have mentioned elsewhere, there was the attempted assault on my grandmother outside her home by a crazed woman and her little children.

I had jokingly invited friends at University of Hartford to come and visit me in the naked city at 45 Irving Street. Not long afterward on one unforgettable evening visiting buddies got treated to an earful and eyeful of that same fat woman out in the middle of the street engaging in a shouting match with her estranged husband, a short, slight man. The new normal had arrived on my street and it wasn't good.

Weirder residents were moving in replacing the stable ones from past years. One woman a couple of doors away was dating an Afro American man which infuriated her brother. The angry brother caught her being dropped off from a date one night and pounced on the man pushing him onto the hood of his car and proceeding to pound him. Scenes like this were becoming nightly events in the hood.

A couple of nights later after returning from a date myself I heard rustling in the bushes next door from the Pietro's yard. Moments later, this same woman, clad only in her night gown, appeared having been chased out of her house by her brother.

Still, life went on in the hood. In the summer, our windows were left open, leaving us vulnerable on the driveway side where the bedroom windows weren't high off the ground, the back window by the kitchen which could be accessed from the porch and the four front windows at porch level. Our kitchen could also be entered through a cellar door—that door, leading outside and seldom locked. No home invasions ever occurred unless you consider the rats that had infested the back wall of my bedroom and could be heard moving around at night. I came and went, usually parking in the backyard, oftentimes returning in the wee hours of morning, without incident, the only fear being of encountering one of those monster rats. No break-ins happened around us either.

As far as the nearby streets were concerned, I often walked home after dark from my job at Aetna Life, taking the Sigourney to Homestead route without any problem.

During this time, President Kennedy was assassinated. It was on a day I didn't have any classes and remember going out into the back yard just after I heard about it, in a daze and commiserating with our next door neighbor, then returning to be glued to the television set for days. The magnitude of his death cannot be fully understood in today's world. My English professor, Henry Grattan, often referred to Jack and Jackie as the king and queen and it did have that feel.

In the fall of 1964, an announcement was made that the two family at 10-12 Irving Street, right next to former mayor DeLucco's house, had been sold to a non-profit corporation that planned to use it as a halfway house for ex-convicts coming out of prison. This purchase may have sounded the death knell for stability in the neighborhood and ignited a storm of protest by residents, especially among women, parents, and property owners.

A woman named Sinatro, the Nicholsons—especially Urania Nicholson, who became the spokeswoman--my aunt Vera, and long-time resident, Murray Cohen opposed its coming. They organized, met and fought it in the courts and on the streets, several of the women demonstrating in front of City Hall. They hired a lawyer and filed a lawsuit, winning an injunction from a wheel chair bound judge who would die a few months later. They received lots of press coverage. It was a wonderful example of real democracy in action.

That fall, commuting daily in a 1956 Mercury entering its death throes, I student-taught at Suffield High School and stayed quite busy preparing classes in Macbeth, Hamlet and John Howard Griffin's *Black Like Me*. But I do recall attending one of the opposition meetings and telling the Hartford Courant reporter, "Let them put it on Mountain Road," in West Hartford which actually was quite appropriate considering the fact that attorney Joe Cooney of privileged Prospect Avenue in the west end represented the Halfway House board.

The case went all the way to the Connecticut Supreme Court where the injunction was overturned. It was a major blow to a diverse and functioning, interracial neighborhood, already shaky, struggling to save itself.

Afterward, the shock waves from this led to more For Sale signs on Irving Street and this time my grandmother, now in her early nineties and after three decades in her home, agreed to post her own. The Silvesters, the elderly couple living above us, soon packed up and moved to West Hartford. Others would follow. In the end she sold both properties to a local realtor for approximately fifteen thousand dollars apiece.

My grandmother announced we--our family, my aunt Vera and uncle Armand St. Pierre and kids, Linda and Donna, and Noni— would all be moving to Noni's two family property at 39 Maplewood Avenue in West Hartford, telephone 523-5344. Our new home was on a beautiful tree-lined street, between Farmington Avenue and the Boulevard, on a bus-line and walking distance to the Center. We took the first floor rent, my grandmother, the St.Pierres, the second. However, their arrival would be delayed until later that fall by renovations to their apartment. There was a small yard and a two car garage with a loft.

That early autumn of 1966 after teaching English each day at East Hampton High School, I drove right to our soon-to- be-new home to paint every room in the late afternoons and evenings, riding in a brand new midnight blue Buick Grand Sport convertible with a white top and interior, payments not to exceed one hundred dollars a month for three years. I was living high.

Once finished there, on the anticipated day of departure, my friend Peter Masaitis and I pulled up at 45 Irving Street in a rented truck and loaded up my family's belongings, leaving behind the less than ten year old blonde furniture used by our roomers—perhaps being already outdated-- and upon completion headed west. That wasn't all we left behind. A box of highly desirable rhythm and blues

78 rpm records from my days working the stock room at Seaboard Distributors was left lying in the cellar and more in the garage.

Being young, I never thought to look back.

Two and a half months after arriving on Maplewood, on January 1, 1967, my grandmother, ninety two years old, died in her own bed at her new home.

Appendices

Forgotten North End History, People & Places

1.   **Adams Inn/Tavern:** Northwest corner, Albany and Blue Hills Avenue, 19th-early 20th century.

2.   **Armory at Pavilion and North Main Streets**

3.   **Baby Hospital:** Mather and Vine Streets, summertime care for sick babies of the poor, mostly from the eastside, on property of Mrs. Walt Goodwin, beginning as a tent operation and advancing to "low broad shacks with everything open and screened from the flies," as described in the Hartford Courant. World War I era.

4.   **Marietta Canty:** 61 Mahl Avenue. Radio, film, television and theater actress and Hartford political activist. Graduate of Northeast Elementary School and Hartford Public High School. Appeared in over forty films: *The Lady in Waiting, Father of the Bride, Bad and the Beautiful, and Rebel Without a Cause,* among them. Marlene Deitrich once dictated that a part be written into a movie of hers, specifically for Marianta.

5.   **Circus Grounds:** Barbour Street, site of present day Wish School and site of the tragic July 6, 1944 Circus Fire, killing 168 people, many of them women and children.

6.   **Connecticut Fair Grounds:** Albany and Blue Hills Avenue close to present day Milford Street, 1860's multi-purpose site for horse races, Ivy League baseball games (Yale vs Harvard) and track meets

7.   **Crown Market:** 620 Albany Avenue, 1940-late 1960's; north end's iconic kosher store

8. **John Egan's childhood home (1939--):** 31 Branford Street. Best high school basketball player in New England in 1957 while at Weaver High, 2nd team All American while at Providence College, leading the Friars to NIT Championship in 1961; played for six NBA teams (Pistons, Lakers, Knicks, Bullets, Cavaliers, Rockets)over eleven years and then coached the Houston Rockets for four seasons.

9. **Totie Field's (a.k.a. Sophie Feldman) childhood home:** 119 Adams Street; Weaver High graduate, late 1940's, nationally known comedian and entertainer.

10. **Fuller Brush Company:** 3580 ½ Main Street

11. **Gentlemen's Riding Park:** situated at Albany and Blue Hills near Milford Street. Baseball field for Yale-Harvard game, place for Buffalo Bill Cody Show annually, 1890's-1911 with upwards of 15,000 attending.

12. **Goodwin Tavern:** (early 19th century – late 1950's inn), corner northwest corner of Irving Street and Albany Avenue. Torn down for a Dunkin Donuts franchise.

13. **Hanging Tree:** northeast side of Goodwin property between Irving and Garden Streets. Site of 1650 hanging of Mary Johnson of Wethersfield accused of witchcraft, second such hanging in New England

14. **Hartford Roller Skating Palace:** 3340 North Main Street

15. **Highland Ice House:** 319 Sigourney Street; also Goldstein's Ice House on Martin Street.

16. **Hebrew Ladies Sheltering Home:** Wooster Street

17. **Bobby Knight's childhood home:** 226 Bellevue Square; at age eighteen, member of 1940's Harlem Globetrotter's team that defeated the then current NBA champions, the Lakers.

18. **Norman Lear's childhood home:** 39 Woodstock Street; King Lear, producer of *All in the Family, Sanford & Sons, Jeffersons, Maude, and Good Times television series*. Weaver, class of 1940.

19.   **Lenox Theater:** located at Albany Avenue and Sterling Street, the neighborhood movie house 1925 – 1970.

20.   **Lewis Billiards:** 1702 North Main Street

21.   **Louis Nye, (a.k.a. Neistat):** 44 Baltimore Street, Weaver High School graduate. Nye's father owned Neistat's Grocery Store, 1360 Albany Avenue, at the corner with Adams. Though his grades at Weaver were so poor he couldn't get into the drama club, he was accepted by the WTIC Radio Players along with Michael O'Shea and Ed Begley. In early television, he became famous for his appearances on the Steve Allen TV Show, after getting his start on the Jack Benny and Jimmy Durante Shows.

22.   **Bessie Fleming Proffit:** 47 Suffolk and 167 Kensington Streets. The Hartford Courant called her "Hartford's First Lady of the Blues." Though not a Hartford native, she lived here for some fifty years. Bessie sang with many all time jazz greats— Fats Waller, Count Basie and Ethel Waters among them, and recorded on Columbia Records.

23.   **Charles Nelson Riley's childhood home:** 18 Enfield Street; actor-producer. Weaver High, class of 1948.

24.   **Silex Company:** nationally known manufacturer of glass coffee makers, 80 Pliny Street

25.   **Udolf's Clothing Store:** 362 Albany Avenue: specialized in clothing for oversized and undersized men, attracting customers from far and wide.

IRVING STREET PEOPLE OF NOTE

Alden Grant Davis: 17 Irving, Civil War veteran, r.i.p., October 28, 1918.

Dominic DeLucco: 20 Irving, World War I veteran, alderman, deputy mayor and twice mayor, the first person of Italian descent in that office.

Albert Maule: (1922-2003) 33 Irving Street, Wharton School of Economics graduate, University of Pennsylvania, Finance Director UCONN Law School, Brigadier General First Company, Governor's Foot Guard, Boy Scouts of America Board of Directors. His son became the first high school graduate of Rocky Hill High School to attend and graduate from Harvard University, later became President of the Chicago Police Board.

Mary Grady Meskill: 6 Irving, First Lady of Connecticut (1971-1975), Thomas Meskill's wife.

Harry O'Neil: 9 Irving, U.S. army veteran, who became a local hero in January of 1919 for saving a fourteen year old boy, Jerry Sullivan, by diving from a bridge under construction fifty feet into the freezing Thames River at New London, only to see the boy die of a head injury the following day.

Robert Simon: (1933-2015), 46 Irving, businessman extraordinaire, Barney School of Business, Simons Real Estate Group's offices spanned several states and includes ones in Atlanta, Houston, Salt Lake City and San Francisco.

Once Upon a Time on
Albany Avenue -- 1955

In the earliest days of the 20th century, Albany Avenue was primarily a growing residential community. Following World War I, however, the Avenue underwent a commercial boom, resulting in a very diversified landscape of small businesses, schools, churches, branch libraries and post offices---public edifices.

By mid-century, Albany was a thriving thoroughfare, bristling with stores, taverns, restaurants, gas stations, drug stores, cleaners, barbers, bakeries and much more, well over two hundred in number.

Among these establishments:

*EIGHT APPLIANCE SHOPS: State Radio near Vine at 706 and Reliable at 860, six others.

*FOUR BAKERIES: Michaels at 240, Pomeranz at 551 near Garden and Baggish, at 1276 near Blue Hills, Mayron's at 1344.

*TWELVE BARBER SHOPS/BEAUTY SALONS: Clay Hill at 447 and Johnny's at 575, ten others.

*TWO BANKS: Riverside at 919 (corner of Cabot) and Society at 1300, near Blue Hills Avenue

*SIXTEEN CLEANERS AND LAUNDRIES: including Thrifty at 629 (near Irving) and Howard at 849, near Burton.

*FOUR CLOTHING: stores: Karp's at 292, Udolf's at 363 and Marco's Shoe Repair at 507 which dabbled in clothing on the side and Lillian's Lingerie Shop at 1050.

*TWELVE DENTISTS AND DOCTORS: Lieberman, Goldenberg, Platt, Mirman and Schuman, Hirshfield, Cohen, Sudarsky, Older, and Weiss, among them.

*SIX DELIS AND LUNCHEONETTES: Platt's, 677 at Magnolia, the Colony at 557, Lenox Coffee Shop at 940, diagonally across from the Lenox Theater, the Edgewood Luncheonette at 851 and two others

*THREE DINERS: Roxy at 444, the Wonder at 560, owned by the Stylle family and the Lasalle, near Homestead.

*NINE DRUG STORES: Madsen's in Clay Hill at 304, Bill Harris (the corner of Garden)at 519, Jacks at 714, on the corner of Vine, Morris Pharmacy, owned by Harry and Morris Feldman, at 721 (Burton Street), McCarthy's at 1005 near the Lenox Theater, plus the popular, Maxwell Drugs at Blues Hills, Maxwell Rulnick, owner, Shermans at 1279, Goursons at 1170, and Baltimore Drug at 1470 Albany Avenue and Baltimore Street.

*TWO FUNERAL PARLORS: Johnson's at 749 and Granstein's at 826.

*SEVENTEEN GAS STATIONS: starting with an Esso station at 215 Albany Avenue, a Merit station at 52, the Gallucci family's station at Garden, number 550, three filling stations at the corners of Irving Street, Carino's at 885, Bilcourt's, 949, at Cabot, Case at 999, Hy's at 1161, Woodland Garage at 1137, and another six stations.

*TWENTY-THREE GROCERY STORES: The Avenue boasted a number of food stores, some big, some tiny with ethic specialties. Crown Market and Irving's Kosher Market catered to the North End's large Jewish population. Smaller operations like Guinta Bros. and Charlie's serviced an Italian clientele. Other noteworthy food establishments: Food Saver at 427, Spinellis at 439, Stop & Shop at 800 near Sigourney, and First National Store at Edgewood and another at Westbourne Parkway. No list could be complete without adding Mott's Supermarket at Harrison Street.

*THIRTEEN RESTAURANTS: among them: The Red Ash at 431, New Deerfield at 463, The Barn at 481, the Garden Restaurant the Grill at 541, White Cedar at 817, Charlies at 978

Many of these establishments typically had liquor licenses and doubled as taverns.

* FIVE SHOE REPAIR SHOPS: Marco's at 507 near Garden was well known.

*FOUR TAVERNS: O'Connors, the Golden Oak with the cane backed chairs near Magnolia, the Blue Hills, the Lenox at Lenox and Pontillo's at 1444.

Besides what's included in this summary, there were numerous other commercial, public and religious institutions:

*Northwest-Jones Junior High School at Woodland and Albany and the nearby Hartford Public

*Library Branch.

*The U.S.Post Office near Woodland Street.

*Horace Bushnell Congregational Church at Vine Street.

*Shiloh Baptist Church located at 350 Albany Avenue

*North Methodist Church at Woodland Street

Some were singular commercial establishments:

*The Lenox Theater at 961 next to Sterling

*Seaboard Record Distributors at 919 Albany Avenue, behind the Stop & Shop, a supplier of 45 and 78 rpm singles.

*Kay's Fish Market at 1450 Albany Avenue

*Lindy's Hardware at Harrison Street

*Dairy Queen at 1287 Albany Avenue

*The Shoe Rack 1229 Albany Avenue

And so many more.

Sources

PREFACE

Hartford Courant: April 27, 1929, February 25, 1945, October 28, 1918, May 5, 1949; Murray Cohen, phone interview, September, 2010

ON THE MOVE

Hartford Courant: January 21, 1940, February 21, 1943, "The Long and Storied Road to Albany," Ellsworth Grant, May 23, 2004; Homestead Park Corporation pamphlet, 1902 (Connecticut Historical Society); "Handsome and Brilliant," phone interview, Margaret Morriarity, May 2009;

"Poems of Rose Sullivan," unpublished, 1930's-1940's; Petition for Naturalization, May 24, 1916, Domenico Laurenzo; Petition for Naturalization, March 19, 1914, Michael J. Sullivan; Hartford City Directory, 1913;

THE CIRCUS FIRE

Interview: J. Gregori Montano, July, 2009; Interview: Sam Testa, May, 1997 conversation; Circus Fire Memories: Survivor Recollections of July 6, 1944, Don Massey, editor, Willow Brook Press, 2006

CHRISTMAS ITALIANO

Taped Interview, Rose Sullivan, December, 1964

ST. JOSEPH CATHEDRAL SCHOOL

"Edgewood Street Tales," Michael J. Angellilo," September, 2015; Anecdote about corporeal punishment, alumni, Grand Reunion, May, 2015; – "Bring Flowers of the Fairest," Mary E. Walsh, 1871/1873, www/catholic tradition.org/rarest: htm; Hartford Courant, December 12, 1981 (Mary Ellen Prout).

51-53

Hartford City Directory 1905-1915, 1920; "Brazilian Years: Conversation with Ziz," August, 2003; "Dadone," Paul Ostiguy, October, 2010; "Chicken Man and Other Stories," Robert Ostiguy, February, 2015; Hartford Courant: Nonni & Mrs. Kaplan, Hartford Courant, September 11, 1926 ("23 in Court Arrested on Vice Charge"); Petition for Naturalization, Michael J. Sullivan, March 19, 1914; Conversation with Donna Nardi, February, 2015.

CHILD OF THE TIMES

Hartford Courant, May 5, 1949 and February 25, 1945; "Chico" by Eileen Sullivan, December, 2014; "The Scout," Michael J. Angellilo, September, 2015, Donna Nardi, March, 2015

BASEBALL

National Italian American Sports Hall of Fame, "Zeke Bonura," www.niashf.org/inductees/zeke-bonura/

THE LENOX THEATER

Hartford Times, April 20, 1973; Hartford Courant: June 7 & 9, 1925, June 19, 1925, January 21, 1926, February 14, 1926, February 28, 1926, 1926, March 7, 1926, March 14, 1926, April 18, 1926, April 25, 1926, May 3, 1926, May 23, 1926, June 6, 1926, June 20, 1926, July 4, 1926, August 1, 1926, August 29, 1926, October 3, 1926, October 17, 1926, December 5, 1926, January 2, 1927, January 30, 1927, February 6, 1927, February 13, 1927, March 27, 1927, April 27, 1927, May 1, 1927, May 2, 1927, May 29, 1927, June 22, 1927, July 3, 1927, November 20, 1927, April 22, 1928, April 29, 1928, September 9, 1928, March 22, 1929, March 31, 1929, May 12, 1929, July 14, 1929, July 28, 1929, November 3, 1929, November 10, 1929,May 11, 1930, March 6, 1932, October 30, 1932, March 2, 1933, March 13, 1933, April 2, 1933, October 19, 1935, November 13, 1935, October 19, 1939, October 31, 1939, December 14, 1939, September 22, 1940, September 29, 1940, December 15, 1940, July 12, 1942, October 1, 1942, June 27, 1943, March 26, 1944, October 28, 1945, July 21, 1946, December 14, 1948, December 12, 1948, January 9, 1951, September 29, 1951, February 7, 1953, March 29, 1953, April 4, 5, and 7, 1957, January 8, 1958, December 21, 1958, August 8, 1959, July 15, 1960, November 16, 1960, December 8, 1960, February 19, 1961, December 30, 1961, January 6, 1963, March 3, 1963, August 31, 1963, November 10, 1963, December 20, 1963, January 25, 1964, November 20, 1964, December 27, 1964,

April 16, 1965, July 30, 1965, October 20, 1966, February 25, 1967, May 29 & 30, 1967, October 28, 1967, February 8, 1968; New York Times, March 16, 2006 (Fred Cohen and Mt. Kilimanjaro); Box Office Magazine, April, 1960; Youtube.com: "Charles Nelson Reilly, The Life of Reilly, Part 12 (Kate Treske)."

THE GANG WAR

Originally published as "Gang War '55" in *Revisiting Our Neighborhoods, Stories from Hartford's Past,* Joan Walden, editor, Jewish Historical Society of Greater, Hartford, 2013; Hartford Courant, May 6, 1955; Hartford Times, May 6-7, 1955, "Police Tip Averts Teen-Age Gang War..."

CHAMPIONS

Input, Bob Countryman, July - November, 2015; Weaver High School yearbooks: 1954, 1955,1956, 1957; Hartford Times: March 9, 1954, March 10, 1954, March 11, 1954, March 13, 1954; Hartford Courant: October 19, 1940 (Charlie Horvath), March 2, 1945, March 15, 1945, August 23, 1945, March 2, 1954, March 12,1954, March 17, 1954, March 19, 1954, June 16, 1954, December 9, 1954, December 12, 1954, December 13 & 14, 1954, December 15, 1954, December 16, 1954, January 23, 1955, January 29, 1955, February 12, 1955, April 6 & 7, 1955, August 10, 1955, September 7, 1955, December 14, 1955, December 16 & 17, 1955, December 21, 1955, January 7, 1956, January 12, 1956, January 15, 1956, January 22, 1956, January 28, 1956, February 1, 1956, February 3, 1956, February 4, 1956, February 11, 1956, February 14 & 15, 1956, February 23, 1956, March 2, 1956, March 4, 1956, March 11 & 13, 1956, March 15, 1956, April 10, 1956, August 11, 1956, December 6, 1956, December 13 & 14, 1956, December 21, 1956, December 28, 1956, January 12, 1957, January 25, 1957, January 30, 1957, February 5, 1957, March 4, 1957, March 8, 1957, March 11, 1957, March 15, 1957; Phone conversation with Joe Cassano, Jr., September, 2015.

THE LIGHT

Classic Urban Harmony.net: " The Valentine's and Alan Freed Halloween Show, October 31, 1955, State Theater, Hartford;" "Mr. DeVaux," Michael J. Angellilo, June, 2015; "Lenox Theater," Tom Shea, email, 2015

EXODUS

Hartford Courant: September 2, 1960, October 2, 1961,October 5, 1961, November 16, 1961, November 29, 1961, December 7, 1961,January 2, 1962, March 5, 1964, October 31, 1964, November 25, 1964,November 29 1964 December 2, 1964,December 19, 1964, December 24, 1964, December 29, 1964.

APPENDICES

Forgotten North End History, People & Places

"Colonial History of Hartford," William De Loss Love, Centinel Hill Press, 1974; "Marianta Canty:www.gov/nr/feature/wom/2002/canty.htm; John Egan: Wikipedia.org, www.friars.com/sports/m-baskbl/../egan; Hartford Courant: "Babies Hospital,"June 17, 1913, "Bessie Proffitt,"June 16, 1957, and March 3, 1973, "Louis Nye," December 9, 1962 and January 1, 1968,"The Long & Storied Road to Albany," Ellsworth Grant, May 23, 2004; Hartford City Directory1930.

Irving Street People of Note

Hartford Courant: October 28, 1918, January 18, 1919, January 10, 2003, February 12, 2015; "Dominic DeLucco Collection," Connecticut Historical Society.

Once Upon a Time on Albany Avenue

Hartford City Directory, 1955, Hartford Public Library